Study Success
A Guide for the Adult Student

By
Janice Raye Stuart

2nd Edition
2010

Photos taken by Bill and Janice Stuart
Cover Design by Tim Stuart*

*2008 Graduate of Durham Technical Community College
Associate in Arts in University Transfer
Associate in Applied Science in Computer Information Technology & Database Management

Student Survival Checklist

For adults, the first few weeks of school can be overwhelming. This is not high school where teachers tell students how to get started. Use the checklist below to prepare for your academic successes. Put a check (✓) when you've completed each task.

	Get your student ID card! It will be necessary to use the college's library, learning center or computer labs. Campus security may ask for your college ID to determine if you belong on campus (which is great since it's your safety they have in mind).
	Get your parking pass or decal
	Check your email. Many colleges offer a student email account, but you must open and use it to activate. Your school will send important information and update via your college email address. Link it to your regular email!
	ORGANIZE YOUR NOTEBOOK. See chapter two on being organized. But for now put all papers in three-ring binder.
	Dedicate a flash drive to your courses this semester. Later in this textbook, you'll learn some useful strategies in saving files. For now, make sure you know how to use a flash drive to save your work and open it on different computers.
	Find your instructors' offices. The absolute worst time to try to find your instructor is when you are in crisis. Put their email addresses in your email and their phone numbers in your cell phone!
	Log into the college's learning management system such as Blackboard, Moodle or Sakai. Depending on your instructor and class format, you may be required to post to the discussion board or submit your assignments on via this system. Many instructors also post lecture notes and handouts online, so if you are absent from class, you can often find useful class materials on your class site.
	Read your course syllabi. Look for your instructors' attendance policies, late policies, and contact information. Also, write assignment due dates and test dates in your weekly planner or calendar, so you will have all of your deadlines in one place.

	Consider your classroom strategies.
	  ☐ Arrive a few minutes early and get your notebook and materials ready for the class's activity.
	  ☐ Sit at the front of the room.
	  ☐ Minimize distractions by turning your cell phone off and sitting away from the door, windows, and chatty classmates.
	  ☐ Come to class prepared mentally and physically.
	  ☐ Participate in class discussions and group work.

Introduction

Welcome, Adult Learner! You have made an important decision to continue your education either in a college or continued education setting. You have brought important experiences, skills and knowledge with you into this program, and you should strive to incorporate those abilities into your studies!

You are to be commended if you are reading this introduction without special directions from your instructor! This means you already possess an important reading skill--previewing. If you've been told to read this introduction, you are still to be congratulated since you have listened to or written down your instructor's directions. In this course, you will learn (or review) many reading and studying skills to guide you through the courses and tests you must complete for your diploma, certificate or degree.

There are many tools in this book to help you with your coursework as well as an exploration of your career choice(s). Do the work, try out the methods and add to your repertoire of skills as you go. You may not remember all the names or titles when you are through, but you should be well practiced to finish your educational journey.

Good luck, and may every class be a success for you!

Janice Raye Stuart
Instructor for Durham Technical Community College

A Note of Thanks...

Thanks to my husband and son, for their aid in formatting the pictures, print and cover. Special thanks to Gabby McCutchen, supervisor for the Study Success program at DTCC and especially to Beatrice Muhammad who helped establish study skills as a necessary course in Basic Skills. Finally, thanks to all the students who have contributed their ideas and experiences that have added and shaped the contents of this text.

GETTING THE MOST FROM THIS TEXTBOOK

This textbook is designed to help the new college student or returning adult learner. There are many skills to try out and inventories to help you discover your strengths (or needs for improvement) as a student striving for success.

Each chapter has informational readings broken into a number of subtopics related to a larger theme. Some sections have both highlighting and annotation practice. Completing these activities with increase two important skills you will need to increase your understanding of college textbooks.

Use a highlighter (yellow is best) to mark the recommended items. Annotation involves your writing in the margins. You will be asked to note personal questions or ideas to compliment the presented information. You could use "sticky" notes in order to write more or to transfer the ideas into your class notes.

Additionally, each chapter will provide "Reflections" for you to apply the information to your personal life as a student. Write the answers to these in a journal or in a special section of your notebook. Think about your answers, and be honest about what you write—there is no right or wrong, and it's not an English exercise.

Finally, there are practicums with scenarios in which you can apply the information. These will increase your critical thinking and ability to "navigate" the college world.

Reading This Textbook

There are many techniques for approaching your textbook reading assignments. Most importantly, remember you are *study reading* as opposed to pleasure reading. Use this easy technique to get more out of your assignments. Use it in conjunction with highlighting and annotation. So, as you begin to work through this text, use this reading technique for best results!

SQ3R: A Reading Technique

Survey

Preview the chapter; look at subtitles, charts, maps, pictures, and questions at the end. You may want to read the summary at the end of the chapter.

Question

✓ What is the chapter about?
✓ What are its main ideas?
✓ What does the instructor want me to know?
✓ Are there items for a test in this chapter?

Read

Read the text carefully. Underline important ideas.

Recite

Rehearse what you've read either orally or in some written form, especially items you underlined or noted. Compare what you know to class notes.

Review

Reread for any details you may have missed or to answer questions at the end of the chapter or given by the instructor.

Always repeat the last two steps, if you cannot answer the questions you created earlier. This will also give you something to share in a class discussion of the material! Now let's get started…

Table of Contents

Chapter 1

College and Lifelong Education
Foundational Information

College Schedule
Personnel
Delivery of Instruction
College Campus

Am I Ready for College or Lifelong Education?

Directions: Check the items that you feel you are personally ready to face in the college atmosphere. Write a question you have in the third column.

Yes No	I am ready to face…	I want to know:
	Adapting to a schedule where my classes aren't "back-to-back."	
	Finding my instructors' offices.	
	Finding the security office.	
	Getting my college ID card.	
	This is NOT like public high school.	
	Adding class time to my job schedule.	
	Buying my textbooks.	
	Applying for and using financial aid.	
	Changing my schedule every 12 to 16 weeks.	
	Getting my parking permit.	
	Finding a parking space where there are none.	
	Finding tutors when I need them.	
	Studying in the library.	
	Taking an online course.	
	Taking more responsibility for my learning than I had to in high school.	
	Scheduling my "free" time to study	
	Socializing less to study	
	Interacting with a new college culture	
	Taking advantage of learning opportunities	
	Preparing for midterms and finals (Oh my!).	

New School...New World

Most likely, you have attended some type of school when you were in high school; this may have been a public school with large classes or a private school with smaller ones. You may have been home-schooled which is more like a private tutorial. You may have just graduated or have attended school very recently, or it may be that you've been out of school for many years. In any of these cases, you are now attending college classes (even if you aren't taking college-level curriculum), and this means you have a whole new set of expectations, requirements and behaviors.

Community colleges are generally two-year colleges (in some places they're called junior colleges) where students strive to get associate degrees, certificates, or diplomas. These areas of study tend to be in technical fields or preparation for transfer for universities and four-year colleges. They include support fields in IT for computers or secretarial science. Students who choose community colleges are looking to complete their studies quickly, so they can go to work in their chosen careers. One student put it like this, "Community colleges are for those who want to get in and get out quickly."

Nowadays, community colleges often provide training for those who need to be retrained in a new career area. These students have been displaced by layoffs or by jobs that have been outsourced to other countries where labor is cheaper. Others come to the community college to get updated in their careers especially as technology continues to advance and change.

Finally, community colleges are both flexible and cost-efficient. Adult students often work full-time, and community colleges have scheduled classes at night or weekends. The student can take one or more classes as they have time. Many colleges have an open-door policy which means the student is not required to have high grades or SAT scores for acceptance; the college gives an entrance test to measure the student's abilities in reading, writing and math. A student who needs improvement will be assigned to developmental classes to improve these skills, so he or she can be successful in college-level coursework. The classes cost less (although books may still be very expensive) which is beneficial for students who must work while going to class or who need financial aid but do not want to borrow large amounts for universities or private colleges. University transfer programs are popular at community colleges which allow students to complete their first two years of general education required by universities. They will earn an associate's degree then move on to earn a bachelor's degree at a four-year college or university.

Community colleges differ from universities or four-year colleges in many ways. The most common difference is that community college students commute from their homes; there is no campus housing. The lack of campus living reduces the social aspects of college life as well. While there may be college clubs, there are fewer social events organized by a typical four-year institution. Students will come to campus, attend classes, study in the library or work in computer labs, but generally they do not stay on campus for long periods of time; thus, they do not socialize as much with other students. Sometimes students find the community college atmosphere more serious or mundane because of the come-and-go workaday schedule of commuting students. This may also contribute to scheduling issues or transportation problems, so students must decide how to best use their time if they ride buses or have gaps in their class schedules. No matter why students choose community colleges, these schools provide great opportunities for education and advancement.

Reflection: Why did you choose to attend a community college?

Your First Day in College

When you arrived (or visited) the first time on campus, did you feel an air of excitement? Or perhaps you felt a bit nervous especially if you just graduated from high school or have been out of school for a while. In either case, there are a few things to make sure you get off to good start. You should carry a few things with you to make sure you're moving in the right direction:

- ☐ A printout of your class schedule
- ☐ A campus map
- ☐ A 3-ring binder (one with pockets) that has paper
- ☐ Two or three ink pens
- ☐ Your student ID (see next pages about that)
- ☐ A parking pass for your car (put it in/on the car)

Come prepared with plenty of time to get to your classes on time. It is not a bad idea to go a day early and actually "walk" the path from the parking lot to your classroom; it is a better idea to park farther away because you probably will not get to park right in front of the building where your class is located. Make a note of places such as a break area or cafeteria and the library which is actually great place to be between classes.

Be confident and interact with other students. You'll be surprised at how many other new students there are, and now is a great time to begin to network. Find out what others are taking and what their programs are. You may be taking similar classes! If the student has been there a while, s/he may be a great source of information about "secrets" of the campus such as a great study place or resource you could use. Students who've been enrolled a few semesters also know about instructors and courses; they are source of information about how to navigate and what are both good and bad practices for college students. Once you're in class, don't be afraid to introduce yourself to the students seated around you. Your classmates may be interested in forming study groups, or you may find out that you need to sit in a different spot where there are more serious students.

Listen to your instructors closely and read all the information they hand out. If they refer you to a website or course link, make sure you go there as soon as possible. The beginning of semester often seems like an easy, light schedule with fewer assignments, but you must realize that you need to start right away and avoid procrastination—the true enemy of students.   Finally, relax. Take some time at home to mull over all that happened and plan the next few days. Your schedule will become busy before you realize it!

College Personnel

Public high schools have different titles for their leaders (principal), teachers, and support personnel. Following is a list of college personnel:

Personnel	Job description	How they help students
System Office	State-level director of system.	Advocate to state government for money and set policies for all community colleges.
Board of Trustees	Community and college leaders who guide college.	Provide community support and monies. Help establish policies.
President	Head of the college.	Represents college and its students to the community.
Vice-President	Assists president.	Various areas can include instruction (so helps guide programs and set standards), or facilities support (physical needs of college and its students)
Dean	Directs a school or program area.	Directs instructors, sets budgets, guides program supervisors.
Program director or department chair.	Directs program areas or classes.	Supervises instructors directly. Can help students work with instructors.
Instructor or professor. (pl. faculty)	Teaches classes and advises students.	Provides instruction, grades work, tutors students, advises students during registration.
Adjunct faculty.	Teach classes part-time.	Provides instruction and grades work. May not have office or advise students.
Registrar	Heads registration.	Takes registration and guides process; provides student records, drop or withdrawal when needed.
Advisor	Advises student. (May also be an instructor)	Sees students prior to registration and provides advice to guide student in his/her program.
Counselor	Provides counseling for students.	Counsels students in educational needs and provides referrals.

Personnel	Job description	How they help students
Security or campus police	Enforces law and investigates campus crimes.	Escorts to cars when needed; enforces parking rules, and keeps campus secure from non-students.
Financial aid officer	Helps students with financial aid.	Helps students fill out FAFSA (Federal requests to determine need for students); helps students access scholarships, loans, or grants.
IT Support	Supports campus computers/servers.	Keep computers and their programs up-to-date. Maintain equipment & monitor Internet use.
Lab Monitor	Supervises computer lab.	Help students use computers and maintain lab for college.
Program Assistant	Office staff for departments.	Interfaces students with deans, supervisors and faculty.
Tutors	Help students in learning centers.	Provide basic tutoring to help student increase skills.
Testing Administrator	Administers tests in testing center.	Manages strict control of standardized college or licensure tests.
Student Senate	Governs the student body	Represents student interests.

It is important to know your college personnel in order to get the help you need. You will interact with many of these important people who will aid you as you navigate through your college program. Learn whom to go to first, so that you do not waste valuable time in your schedule. For instance, if you have a problem with an instructor, you should first speak to your instructor (see Chapter 3 for information on being assertive and communicating effectively) in a private setting such as after class or in his/her office. If your issue cannot be resolved, then you may want to go his/her supervisor or department chair. The next person in this chain, would be the program's dean (or assistant dean if your college is organized that way). Your highest authority at the college is a last resort. Although every college president is deeply concerned with the success of the students, s/he is also one of the busiest people. Whenever you "jump" over rungs in the leadership hierarchy, you will be asked did you consult the lower rungs first. Don't be afraid, but always be planned in whom you consult to solve educational issues.

Reflection: How do you feel when you need to ask for help? Do you feel confident in finding the right person to answer your questions? Who else can you ask?

Practicum Discussion

Review each scenario and decide what action(s) that the student should take to resolve his or her problem or need.

Scenario 1:

John had an individualized learning plan while he was in public schools. His plan gave him accommodations in areas such as testing and class instructional materials. As a first semester student, John has begun his classes and found he struggles with how the materials are presented in the classroom. He is afraid that he will not do well on the upcoming test. What should John do? Whom should he see? What should he ask?

Scenario 2:

Susie's advisor did not advise her that the course she is currently enrolled actually is the same course (with a different course number and listing) she took two years ago when she first enrolled at the college. She passed the course then with a solid C average. She feels frustrated because it is the same material that what covered previously. She discovers this after the first day of class after the instructor reviews the course outline, objectives and syllabus. What should Susie do? Whom should she go to?

Scenario 3:

Mark completed his first major assignment in his English class but is not sure if it meets the requirements set forth by the instructor. The assignment is due in two days (it's not the weekend) and he worries he will fail the assignment. He spoke with the instructor about an earlier assignment he had turned in late and felt that the instructor was not as approachable as his high school teachers. What should Mark do now? What might have Mark done before?

Scenario 4:

Jan had to clarify with the registrar's office about an earlier failed course. This resulted in her not being about to register early of which she was informed by a letter. Now it is the final day to register, and she has been told by the registrar's office that she has to come back to late registration day (which will cost a fee). She had to get her husband to leave work early, so she had someone to take care of the baby and would have the car to use; this change will make it impossible to come to late registration. What should Jan do? Is there someone she can talk to in order to rectify the matter on this last day of general registration?

Campus Locations

A college campus is generally spread over several buildings although some very small colleges may only occupy a single building. Some colleges have a main campus and satellite campuses. Community colleges often serve several counties or towns and either use a satellite campus or community sites such as public schools, churches, community centers or business places for classes. Check your registration schedule for details and abbreviation codes to locate classes. There are some general places every student should be aware of:

Place/department	Activity	How it helps students
Registrar's office	Registration files	Turn in registration, change class schedule, drop or withdraw from classes.
Business office	Payments	Pay for classes or fees at this location.
Counseling	Campus counselors' offices and space	See counselor or go for de-stressing (quiet space).
Advisor's or instructor's office	Located in various buildings	Go for tutoring, talking to instructor and turning in work (NEVER leave work in your classroom!!)
Labs	Special work or instructional space	Some computer labs are open (bring ID). Other labs for science or technology.
Quad or plaza	General green space	Gathering place or used for large campus events
Auditorium	Large space for meeting or classes	Guest speakers, program events.
Learning Center	Tutoring	Meet with tutors
Testing Center	Standardized Testing	Special testing for entrance or licensure. Very quiet, restricted area.
Department Office	Staff offices/dean	Meet with support staff for programs.
ESL Office	Supports classes for foreign students needing basic English	Students who need basic instruction register here

Student Services	Building or space for registrar, advising, counseling, etc.	One-stop space for student registration, records and advising
Campus Bookstore	Textbook distribution	Buy books here!
Cafeteria	Food!	May have hot food or just vending.
Student Lounge	Located in various buildings	Space to relax or study. May have vending and copier.
Library or Educational Resource Center	For research and study.	Ask for help with research. Check out books. Get copies.
Reserve Desk	Located in library	Many instructors have copies of textbooks or other resources. Can be used in library only.

Get a map of your campus to locate each of these services. Plan plenty of time to park since parking is ALWAYS busy on EVERY campus. You will probably need a parking permit, along with your college ID card, so get this in your campus security office.

Special Note About ID Cards: Check to see whether you must renew parking permits and ID cards on a semester basis. Carry your ID for purposes of security checks, computer or other lab access and library privileges. You may be asked to produce your ID in order to take tests and register as well. Finally, college ID cards can have special "perks" in the everyday world such as college discounts at theaters or sports events and for purchases given by local merchants to encourage college students to use their services/products.

STUDY SKILL PRACTICE: Look at the above chart and **highlight** places you've used so far this semester. Then **annotate** in the margin one place you need (or will in the near future) to access. Write down a question you think would need to ask personnel once you're there!

Instructional Delivery

The college offers instruction in a variety of ways. Make sure you understand how your program provides students training and information for their programs.

General classes are often referred to as "lecture" format. This is the setting where an instructor teaches the body of students. Lectures may include verbal instruction, discussions, presentations and demonstrations. There may be films or videos as well as activities for students to practice skills they have been taught or studied in textbooks. Some courses are offered **online** or as **hybrids** (mixed online and on-site classes). Be aware that online and hybrid courses are not easier versions of on-site classes; in fact, these course require more hours to complete because the online activities are intense and designed to cover material as thoroughly as an instructor would in a classroom setting. Time may be required to participate in scheduled online discussions or interaction with the instructor and other members of a class just as if meeting in person.

Labs may be required for students to take in conjunction with a class. These are activity-based instruction and practice for students to help them perform skills. Language and science classes most often have labs, but in programs such as technology-based areas, there are also required labs. Beware that the student must pass BOTH the lab and its lecture component in order to get credit (or a particular grade of "C" or better may be required). Labs can also be taught by a second instructor! They may also require special fees and materials. You may have to register for the lab component separately, so check your course registration numbers.

Practicums or clinicals are special courses designed around practice in career areas. Nursing students, for instance, may take clincals that meet several hours each week in a special setting such as a hospital. Students may be required to purchase uniforms or equipment. There is usually a stricter attendance requirement.

Co-oping is also common. Often completed the last semester in a program, this is could be considered a "practice" job in which students gain valuable on-the-job training. There is usually no pay in co-op courses, and students register for these classes just like others. In many cases, the student must have a *resume* to be placed in the best co-op position as possible.   This experience-based course will allow students to tell future employers they have had real-world work experience in their career.

Look at the following plan of study and courses listed:

Spring Semester

	Course	Class	Lab/shop	Clinical/co-op	Credit
BIO 166	**Anatomy and Physiology II**	3	3	0	4
BIO 175	**General Microbiology**	2	2	0	3
PED 110	**Fit and Well for Life**	1	2	0	2
PSY 281	**Abnormal Psychology**	3	0	0	3
SOC 213	**Sociology of the Family**	3	0	0	3

Source: http://www.forsythtech.edu/catalog/1011/program/associate-in-arts-pre-major-nursing

As you look at this *plan of study*, notice that there are three columns that show what <u>hours</u> each week are required in class, lab or shop and clinical or co-op. A student must add together these columns to plan how many hours a week a course will meet. The credit column shows how many credit hours the student will earn. In the above example, the student will spend a total of 19 hours a week in class and lab; however, s/he is only earning 15 hours of credit.

As a community college student, be prepared for all types of instructional and learning experiences!

Practice:

Write the courses you are taking this semester, the hours you meet in class and lab or shop. Fill in the credit hours you are receiving. Then total. Are they equal? Finally estimate how much time you must spend studying for each week. (Note: if you have an online course, you will need to schedule 3 to 4 hours a week per credit hour you will earn for the course—later you may realize this may need to be MORE).

Course #	Course Title	Class Hrs.	Lab/Shop Hrs.	Credit

Additional copies of this form are found in the last appendix. Find your plan of study and plot out your future semesters!

The College Schedule

Most colleges operate on a **semester** plan; there are two 15-17 week periods yearly, one in fall and one in spring. A short summer term may be offered but lasts only six to ten weeks. A few colleges operate on quarter system in which each term lasts nine to twelve weeks.

A registration period is open prior to the first week of classes. The college will publish a course schedule for the next semester (usually both on paper and online). It is important to make an appointment with your advisor **immediately** when early registration is set. You will need to meet with him/her to get your PIN number to register by phone or computer OR to get his/her signature of approval if registration is done on paper. Keep a copy of your schedule in a safe place (a new notebook or in your wallet). Review your schedule prior to attending and plan to ATTEND the first day. You will need to pay by the payment-due date in order to avoid having your schedule cancelled, thus losing your reserved class seat!

The first day of classes for each class is essential. This is not like public high school where the first day seems superfluous. The instructor or professor will go over vital information such as your syllabus, course requirements, testing, grade weights, attendance requirements and your first assignment for the very next class. After the class meets, go over all the handouts and be prepared to ask any questions you have during the next class or contact the instructor before the next class.

A **HYBRID** course is one that meets **both** online and in a physical class. The first meeting is always in the classroom before the online component begins. You must attend the on-site classes as well as do work online. A strictly online course generally has a face-to-face orientation with the instructor. Talk to your advisor if you're unsure of where to go for your hybrid or online course.

Many colleges have a **drop/add day** on which you can change your course schedule. There a withdrawal dates on which you can submit paperwork to withdraw without a penalty or get a refund. You must meet the deadline or a grade of F or F2 (lack of attendance) will be submitted by the instructor.

Some colleges have an exam period and a reading day (no classes on that day, just for studying). Make sure you follow that schedule closely.

Look for other important dates by accessing the "Academic Calendar" online for your college; in some cases, this may be published in the registration schedule (paper version). Watch for e-mails from your college (see e-mail information in research section of this book) that announce important dates. Write important dates on a paper calendar and in your planner.

There are also other activities on campus. Many colleges have a fall festival or spring festival when college clubs have information and activities for the student body. There may be free food and prizes at these events and often faculty participate in these gatherings. Additionally, colleges offer seminar and arts activities for students. These are free and provide opportunities for students to discuss new ideas and get the latest information on research and discoveries in science, technology, medicine or the arts. If students are creative, there may be drama productions, a college newspaper, art displays, or a college creative writing journal to participate in. College organizations and clubs are great ways to expand career networking. There may be job fairs on campus or college recruiters for transfer students. Finally, there may be a student senate that meets; students may attend or act as representatives in this governing body.

Take advantage of these education-building activities! You may never have so much fun!

Reflection: What kind of activities would you enjoy or benefit from attending?

Plan of Study or What Classes Do I Take?

Whatever career track a student chooses, there will be some classes that he or she must take to add to his/her career-success skills. If the entrance assessment indicates skills improvements, a student will be required to take **developmental** classes to build skills such as reading, writing, or mathematics. These skills are essential for any academic success and must be completed BEFORE the student begins his/her program of study.

Additionally, all career areas require general education classes (not developmental but college-level) such as writing, speech-making, critical thinking, psychology, computer use, or math. These vary by program yet are the building blocks to success in various careers. For instance, a nurse will need to communicate both verbally and written, so he or she will take English composition and speech to prepare. A nursing student will take classes in medicine, so he or she will need college Algebra, chemistry and biology to prepare. Patients have emotional or mental responses to their illnesses, so the future nurse will need psychology. These would all be classes taken before actual nursing classes.

So how does a student know what to take? The first time he or she registers, a temporary advisor will help by going over the **PLAN OF STUDY** for a particular program chosen by the student. The advisor will also help the student register for developmental classes indicated by the entrance tests. Later, students get an advisor in his/her chosen program. It is essential that the student meet with the advisor on a regular basis especially prior to registration or any time he or she needs to change a class schedule or does not complete a necessary course. Most colleges have the plan of study for each program posted online or listed in the college's catalogue or handbook. Look at these closely, for they give a time-plan as well as the required courses. Also, students may need to consider whether they can actually follow the plan if they need extra classes or take fewer than the recommended classes.

Finally, some classes have **pre-requisites** that must be taken <u>before</u>. Other classes have required **co-requisites** which are taken at the same time. Most advisors recommend that these kinds of course be strategically planned to help students maximize contact hours. Note that while many courses have a three or four hour a week schedule, co-op or clinical courses meet for significantly more hours each week and carry more credit hours. Students pay for the number of credit (or semester hours for which they register). Always double check to see if the contact (meeting) hours are the same as credit hours.

The University Transfer Program

As stated earlier, some students choose to do their first two years of a bachelor's degree at the community college. A bachelor's degree is not just training for a career; it reflects more general education for its holder. Unlike other community college students, university transfer students are not taking classes directly related to their career degree (Although a pre-med student might take more science or someone seeking a bachelor of arts will take more social sciences or humanities). The career training will continue once the student transfers and begin his/her junior year at the four-year school. Universities and other four-year colleges offer both a bachelor's of science (BS) and a bachelor's of arts (BA), depending upon field of study. Once a student gets his/her bachelor's, he or she may choose to go on to a master's degree or even doctorate degree.

A bachelor's degree will first require two years of general education in various fields of study. At a typical four-year school, these are done when the student is an undergraduate freshman (first year) and sophomore (second year). The plan of study will include many courses such as English (2-3 courses), math (2-3 classes), science (2 courses with labs), a foreign language (2 courses), humanities (in various areas of art or general studies), as well as social sciences and history (4 courses). The university transfer student will earn approximately half (about 60-64 hours) of his degree at the community college.

In some states, there is an agreement between the community colleges and the state's university system about which courses are acceptable for transfer. In North Carolina, this is called the "**Comprehensive Articulation Agreement**" which outlines courses accepted from the community colleges into the UNC system. Students should make sure they take the correct courses that meet these requirements; otherwise, the university may not accept all courses taken. It is generally best to complete the associate's degree in university transfer BEFORE transferring. The application to enter a university can be submitted in the last semester of community college work. The advisor or a transfer support advisor can help the student through the process. Potential university transfer students should spend time researching their university choices!

Course Requirements

On your first day of class, you should receive a list of requirements for each class you are taking. The list should include:

- o Course objectives (outline of what you will learn)
- o Weight of grades (percentages)
- o Homework and assignment policy
- o Testing
- o Projects
- o Textbooks and assignments
- o Attendance requirements
- o Class rules (optional to instructor)

Go over your handouts and jot down any questions you may have so that you can ask them at your next class meeting. Keep all handouts and **syllabi** for future reference. A **syllabus** (plural: syllabi) is a quarterly or semester plan of class assignments and the dates on which these will be covered.
Put your syllabus in the front of your notebook and check it every class for assignments and topics; you can use the topic list to create subtitles for your note pages. Treat these handouts as you would with any important papers, and **don't throw anything out until you've finished the course** and received a grade.

You will need to use a calendar and/or an assignment sheet (example in this book) to keep up with your course requirements. One of the most effective ways to stay organized is to WRITE down your assignments. Additionally, you may want to add them to your computer calendar system or PDA (personal data assistant).

Always be prepared for changes which is a good reason for not getting behind. A shift in an instructor's syllabus could end up in a "collision" of work due!

What Students Say...

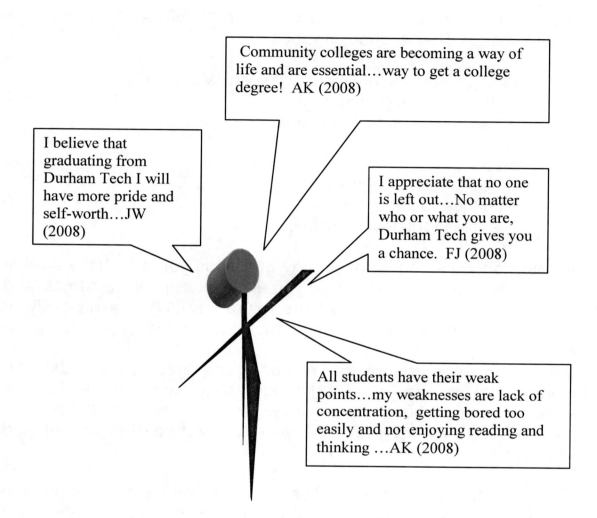

Community colleges are becoming a way of life and are essential…way to get a college degree! AK (2008)

I believe that graduating from Durham Tech I will have more pride and self-worth…JW (2008)

I appreciate that no one is left out…No matter who or what you are, Durham Tech gives you a chance. FJ (2008)

All students have their weak points…my weaknesses are lack of concentration, getting bored too easily and not enjoying reading and thinking …AK (2008)

Chapter 2

Tools for Success

Success
Goals
Attitudes
Time Management
Communication

First Things First

So where would you begin in your mental journey as a college student? A survey taken by Noel-Levitz, Inc., examined three areas of importance to entering college students. Read each and decide which one best describes you:

	I have a very strong desire to continue my education, and I am quite determined to finish a degree.
	I am very strongly dedicated to finishing college—no matter what obstacles get in my way.
	I am deeply committed to my educational goals, and I'm fully prepared to make the effort and sacrifices that will be needed to attain them.

Notice that this survey looks at three factors that will affect your success or persistence (ability to persevere) in college. You will need a few tools for success:

- Values
- Attitude
- Goals

You will want to decide on a career goal in order to see how your education will be an asset. You will want to look at personal goals and expectations.

Once you have goals, you will need a plan of action that will include time and study management. There are a number of assessments, surveys and inventories in this book to help you examine your choices, skills and attitudes. Finally you will need tools and techniques to carry out your plan. This course will help you begin on the right foot and stay on the right track.

Reflection writing:

1. Can you think of other factors that will affect your education?

2. What other resources or skills do you need in order to be successful?

Study Success

You may be wondering, or already done so, why you've been asked to take a college success class. You've managed to make it to school. You've registered for classes. Perhaps you've even purchased all your books. Yet, you also know education is much more than these activities.

Education is more than sitting in class and completing a required set of assignments. When an adult returns to school, education becomes a part of a many-faceted life! Education affects your time, your family, your job, your self-image and your attitudes. You may have even experienced some failure, but with the skills you learn in this course you should be able to turn failure into success.

Think about the word "success" and create a positive picture of the adventure on which you are about to embark. Now complete the acrostic below in which the letters in the word "success" begins each line of the poem. (Hint: don't worry about rhymes!)

S _____

U _____

C _____

C _____

E _____

S _____

S _____

Sharing Interaction. Now share your acrostic about returning to school (or starting college classes) with a classmate.

Following are some sayings and writings about success. Use them to inspire yourself as you face the challenge of being an adult student!

Success

To laugh often and much; to win the respect of intelligent people and the affection of children
to earn the appreciation of honest critics and endure the betrayal of false friends;
to appreciate beauty, to find the best in others;
to leave the world a bit better, whether by a healthy child, a garden patch or a redeemed social condition;
to know even one life has breathed easier
because you have lived.
This is to have succeeded.

Ralph Waldo Emerson

What others have said about success...

"Most successful men have not achieved their distinction by having some new talent or opportunity presented to them. They have developed the opportunity that was at hand."— **Bruce Barton**

"There are three ingredients in the good life: learning, earning and yearning." —**Christopher Morley**

"Success doesn't come to you...you go to it." —**Marva Collins**

"The difference between a successful person and others is not a lack of strength, not a lack of knowledge, but rather in a lack of will." —**Vincent T. Lombardi**

"Success is a journey, not a destination." --**Ben Sweetland**

If you care at all, you'll get some results. If you care enough, you'll get incredible results. --**Jim Rohn**

"Desire is the key to motivation, but it's the determination and commitment to an unrelenting pursuit of your goal - a commitment to excellence - that will enable you to attain the success you seek." **Mario Andretti - race car driver**

"The most practical, beautiful, workable philosophy in the world won't work - if you won't." --**Zig Ziglar**

"Unless you change how you are, you will always have what you've got." --**Jim Rohn**

"Success is not permanent. The same is also true of failure." --**Dell Crossword**

"Success often comes to those who have the aptitude to see way down the road." --**Laing Burns, Jr.**

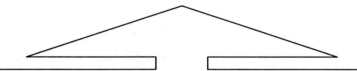

Study Skills Practice: Go back to the previous sayings and **highlight** qualities that contribute to success. **Annotate** in the margin about three of those qualities you either possess now or wish to possess—tell how you will use each!

There are many skills, which may not be study skills, that help you succeed in your life activities of which education is now a part. Following are several lessons on self-esteem, being assertive, communicating and goal setting. Consider each and do the activities! You'll find success will be yours!

Reflection Writing: Briefly describe one event (ANY!) in which you felt successful. How did you feel?

Why is Self-Esteem Important?

Students need a healthy outlook about themselves. How someone views him/herself affects every aspect of life, but the educational setting can be particularly challenging. In this environment, students must face many hurdles that often have strong mental and emotional ups and downs. Here students compare themselves to classmates who may seem smarter or quicker, or they look in the mirror of competency that the course or instructor sets up for measurement. The adult learner may feel his or her whole future is tied into grades or program completion. Education impacts how adults earn and provide for their families and how their goals and values are met. It is important to remember what one First Lady, Eleanor Roosevelt, said, "No one can make you feel inferior without your consent." Mrs. Roosevelt was a trendsetter and social leader who knew what women and minorities faced, but her statement is true of anyone who has faced tasks that often influence his/her self-image.

The definition of **Self Esteem** is how a person sees him/herself. The view includes how a person sees him/herself as lovable and capable. Self-esteem can be either high or low depending how a person sees him/herself and how he or she thinks others see him/her. In *Webster's Unabridged Dictionary* (1983), self-esteem is "belief in oneself; self-respect."

Annotation Practice: How do we develop our view of ourselves? List your ideas in the right-hand margin.

Why is **positive** self-esteem important? Jean Illsley Clarke in her book, *Self-Esteem: A Family Affair* (1978), states, "Positive self-esteem is important because when people experience it, they feel good and look good, they are effective and productive, and they respond to other people and themselves in healthy, positive, growing ways."

Highlight: Go back to Clarke's statement about positive self-esteem and **highlight** all the good, positive words she uses.

Self-Esteem is unique to every individual! No two people see themselves the same way, but every individual can feel good about who he or she is!

My Declaration of Self-Esteem

I AM ME!
I was uniquely created by god. There's not another human
being in the whole world like me--I have my very own fingerprints and I have my
very own thoughts. I was not stamped out of a mold like a Coca-cola top to be
the duplicate of another.

I own all of me--my body, and I can do with it what I choose; my mind, and all of
its thoughts and ideas; my feelings, whether joyful or painful.

I own my ideals, my dreams, my hopes, my fantasies, my fears.

I reserve the right to think and feel differently from others and will grant to others
their right to thoughts and feeling not identical with my own.

I own all my triumphs and successes. I own also my failures and mistakes. I am
the cause of what I do and am responsible for my own behavior. I will permit
myself to be imperfect. When I make mistakes or fall, I will know that I am not
the failure--I am still okay--and I will discard some parts of me that were unfitting
and will try new ways.

I will laugh freely and loudly at myself--a healthy self-affirmation.

I will have fun living inside my skin.

I will remember that the door to everybody's life needs this sign:

HONOR THYSELF.

I have value and worth.
I am me, and I am okay.

(Adapted from Virginia Satir, noted psychotherapist d. 1988)

Roles and Expectations

Adults play many roles every day. These include mother, father, husband, wife, friend, worker, co-worker and others. When an adult returns to the education setting, he or she plays new roles including student and teacher.

The adult learner or student has certain expectations he or she wants from the education arena. The facilitator or instructor is often central to helping the student gain as much as possible in the educational setting. Since these roles are reciprocal*, expectations of the student must be met by certain obligations of the instructor or **facilitator**.

Additionally, an instructor has expectations of the student which entails that the student meet obligations in order to complete a course or acquire competencies the course requires. Look at the chart on the following page and write a list of the expectations you have of this course. Then, write down the obligations you feel the instructors has to meet your expectations. Then reverse the process, and write down the expectations your instructor has and your obligations. Use this as a guide over the semester in how well you and the instructor are proceeding in meeting these obligations and expectations.

*re-cip-ro-cal adj.
   1. Concerning each of two or more persons or things.
   2. Interchanged, given, or owed to each other.
   3. Performed, experienced, or felt by both sides.

College Roles and Expectations

Expectations	Obligations
Instructor	Student
Instructor	Student
Obligations	Expectations

Rewards and Accomplishments

How do you view your rewards? Synonyms of **reward** include *prize, payment, return, incentive, gift*. We can think of rewards in many forms and for many reasons. Let's explore your personal views.

Reflection. Write down three ways you have been rewarded for work you have achieved or completed.

Now look at your list. Did one of your rewards include money? If not, think about how you are rewarded as an employee. You earn money! You are **paid** for work completed.

Reflection. Now list 3 rewards you get in education.

Now look at this list. Did it include grades or points? If not, it should! The pay you get for completing work in a course should include a grade. Of course, there are many intangible, emotional and intellectual rewards you get, but more often students are concerned about the grade. Consider that pay, when you put your effort towards your class-work or homework. Would an employer pay for incomplete or poorly done tasks?

The rest of these lessons will help you become the best educational "worker" you can.

Instructors, Students and Grades

As stated earlier, students earn grades. Occasionally, you might hear a student thank his/her instructor for a good grade, but the student has *earned* the grade. Instructors are guided by a grading scale established by the college or its departments. Some colleges use a ten-point scale where 90-100 is an A, 80-89 is a B and so forth. Others use a seven-point scale:

Numerical	Letter Grade	GPA Points
93-100	A	4
85-92	B	3
77-94	C	2
70-76	D	1
69 & below	F	0

A program may elect not to accept a grade lower than a B or C in order to assure student competency. The GPA represents a student's *grade point average* which continues to change as the student completes courses. The GPA is totaled as follows:

1. Credit hours of course multiplied by points earned to find the quality points a student earned
2. Quality points for all courses are added together and divided by the number of credit hours taken
3. GPA is final number

Example:

Course	Credit hours	Grade	Quality points earned
Math 070	4	B	4 x 3 = 12
English 111	3	A	3 x 4 = 12
ACA 122	1	A	1 x 4 = 4
Biology 111	4	C	4 x 2 = 8
	Total hrs: 11	**Total:**	36 points divided by 11 = 3.27

In the example, the student has an overall GPA for the semester of 3.27 which is a B. The points and GPA continues to accumulate as the student continues to take courses. If one course is failed, the resulting zero points would dramatically affect the overall GPA.

Some colleges may reward variable degrees of each letter grade such as a B+ or B- which will come with more or less points. The instructor will generally give numerical grades between 100 and 0, but reports the grade as an A, B, C, D or F. Courses that are withdrawn or dropped are not added into the GPA. Colleges have different policies about courses that are repeated for higher or passing grades, but the grades usually remain on the student's transcripts.

Instructors assign weights or points to assignments, projects and exams taken during the course. You should examine the course syllabus for clear guidelines which vary by instructors and courses. **Rubrics** (grade checklist for an assignment) help instructors to grade fairly or objectively. A rubric is usually given to the students so they can check their work for completeness and quality.

Grade Weights for a Course	
10%	Homework
20%	Attendance
30%	Project
20%	Unit Tests
5%	Pop Quizzes
15%	Final Exam
-5 pts/day for late assignments	
Pop quizzes cannot be made up	

Essay Rubric Example

Content
Thesis — -8 if missing
Support
Paragraphs — -15 for each missing
Conclusion — -15 if missing
More support or
Detail needed — -3 to -10

Grammar Errors	
Fragments	-4 each
CS or RO	-5 each
Spelling	-3 each
S-V agr.	-3 each
PN ref	-3 each
Punctuation	-2 each

A student's GPA is important for many reasons. If you are transferring to a four-year institution, then your GPA will be a deciding factor in your acceptance into a program. For instance, the University of North Carolina at Chapel Hill requires a minimum of 3.2 for transfer, but competitive programs such as nursing require a 3.5 or higher. If you are planning to go on to graduate school, your major's GPA will also be essential to meet entrance requirements. Finally, a few employers may look at your college transcripts as they evaluate your skills for hiring.

Grade Calculations Practice

1. George made a B in English 111 (3 credits), an A in ACA 122 (1 credit), a C in Biology 150 (4 credit hours) and a B in Math 170 (3 credit hours). What is his GPA?

2. Sue 's course has the following weights: 20% attendance; 30% Portfolio project; 10% Problem-Solution Paper; 15% Final Exam and 25% for Homework assignments. If she makes the following grades, what would be her grade for the course? (HINT: don't convert to decimals; take added total and move decimal left until you have a number.)

	Grade	X	Weight	Total
Portfolio	90			
Attendance	95			
Problem-Solution Paper	80			
Exam	85			
Homework	75			
			Add +	
			Course	

3. Sue's attendance grade drops to 80%. How does that affect her overall grade?

4. If Sue had five homework assignments, but turned in only four. Her grades are the following: 95, 100, 100, and 90. What is her total homework grade? How does that impact her course grade?

5. Look at these four semesters' grades and total an overall GPA:

Fall 10	Credits	Grade	Fall 11	Credits	Grade
ACA 122	1	A	HIS 122	3	A
ENG 111	3	B	PED 150	1	C
BIO 165	4	C	BIO 166	4	B
PSY 150	3	B	PSY 241	3	C
CIS 110	4	A	MAT 162	3	A
Spring 11			**Spring 12**		
ENG 112	3	B	FRE 111	4	F
HIS 121	3	C	HIS 131	3	A
MAT 161	4	B	GEO 111	3	C
HUM 110	3	C	HUM 115	3	C

Personal Mission Statement

A mission statement represents the goals or objectives a company or college has. Each college states its mission statement in its catalogue.

"Durham Technical Community College's mission is to enrich students' lives and the broader community through teaching, learning, and service." (http://www.durhamtech.edu)

All the classes, learning opportunities, services and outreach are based on the college's mission statement. Other colleges or universities will have different mission statement, so look this up for any other school you are considering.

NOW, consider those people and activities you have a commitment to. Consider the goals you have. Now you're ready to write your own personal mission statement.

My Personal Mission Statement:

On the following page, there is a writing called "Desiderata." It could be considered a type of mission statement. Read it and consider its appeal. Highlight words that would be important to a person's goals and values. Are there words that you would include in your life's mission statement? Adults have always been driven by a vision of their future. After you've decided on the wording of your mission statement, type it up and print it out. Post it somewhere you can view it often as you try to succeed in the work and study of your education.

The mission statement you create now may not be the one you will use after college or after events in your life help you grow and mature, but it should reflect your mission now as a student. As you grow older and your life changes, remember to look back at this statement periodically to see if you are following it or whether you need to adjust it.

Desiderata

Go placidly amid the noise and haste, and remember what peace there
may be in silence.
As far as possible without surrender be on good terms with all persons.
Speak your truth quietly and clearly, and listen to others, even the dull and
ignorant; they too have their story.
Avoid loud and aggressive persons; they are vexatious to the spirit.
If you compare yourself with others, you may become vain and bitter; for always
there will be greater and lesser persons than yourself.
Enjoy your achievements as well as your plans.
Keep interested in your own career, however humble; it is a real possession in
the changing fortunes of time.
Exercise caution in your business affairs; for the world is full of trickery.
But let this not blind you to what virtue there is; many persons strive for high
ideals; and everywhere life is full of heroism.
Be yourself.
Especially, do not feign affection.
Neither be cynical about love; for in the face of all anxiety and disenchantment it
is perennial as the grass. Take kindly the counsel of the years, gracefully
surrendering the things of youth.
Nurture strength of spirit to shield you in sudden misfortune. But do not distress
yourself with imaginings.
Many fears are born of fatigue and loneliness.
Beyond a wholesome discipline, be gentle with yourself.
You are a child of the universe, no less than the trees and the stars; you have a
right to be here.   And whether it is clear to you, no doubt the universe is
unfolding as it should . Therefore be at peace with God, whatever you conceive
Him to be, and whatever your labors and aspirations, in the noisy confusion of
life keep peace with your soul.
With all its sham, drudgery and broken dreams it is still a beautiful world. Be
cheerful. Strive to be happy.

--Max Ehrmann, 1927

Values

A value is defined as "the quality (positive or negative) that renders something desirable." (dictionary.com) This word originates from the French term that means "strong," so a value is something that is desired **strongly**.

Just like self-esteem, our values are shaped by many factors such as family, life events, media, education, mentors, friends, religion and society as a whole. What you value shapes your goals and attitudes (discussed next).

If you've chosen to pursue education, it is a given that you VALUE education. You should have a strong desire to gain education. You may have chosen education because you value money or value status or a particular career. These are all personal values and should remain such no matter what your friends and family may think or say.

Your community college has values as well. These are the standards by which it governs the students and faculty. These values may have developed through administrative suggestions, the college system's requirements and/or the community's desires and needs. Here is a list from one community college:

"Our core values are as follows:

- ☐ WELCOMING: We value a welcoming, vibrant, and safe campus environment.
- ☐ LEARNING: We value learning through rigorous quality instruction, focused student support, and appropriate student activities.
- ☐ ENGAGING: We value an engaging, collegial atmosphere with professional, ethical, and respectful interactions that enhance learning.
- ☐ UNDERSTANDING: We value the unique experiences of individuals and the diversity of the community.
- ☐ IMPROVING: We value continual improvement in all areas of the college through encouraging effective innovation, appropriate use of technology, responsible stewardship of financial and human resources, and professional development for faculty and staff.
- ☐ UNIFYING: We value unity through the common purpose of serving students and the community." (www.durhatech.edu)

These values can be seen through programs offered, college rules, and course instruction and competencies. Your personal values will guide you in your choices, your goals and the motivation that drives you to succeed.

Fill in the following table with five of your values and how each one relates to how you conduct your life or choices (an example is given):

Value	How affects life/choice
Trust	*I tell the truth in all matters, so I can be trusted. I want to work with trustworthy people.*

Values in work and education are part of ethics. It is important to learn the ethics code of your career!

Educational Ethics

The educational arena is one of strong ethics. Faculty and students are expected to practice the highest levels of honesty and hard work. At the United States Military Academy at West Point, the code of honor can be summarized as "I will not lie, cheat or steal or tolerate those who do." (cs.uchicago.edu) Note, that this is also quoted as part of the honesty statement students must sign at the University of Chicago!

This standard is part of what earning a degree is about; a degree, diploma or certificate from a college signifies that the holder (student-earner) has the skills that he or she has been educated to possess and use. Unfortunately, plagiarism is a growing concern among all student populations. Often (due to social or cultural differences) some students are confused about what plagiarism (unauthorized copying) is. A typical college's policy for academic honesty may look like this one:

> "Durham Technical Community College demands complete academic integrity from each student. Academic dishonesty is the participation or collaboration in specific prohibited forms of conduct. Participation or collaboration may be active (such as submitting a term paper which includes plagiarized work) or passive (such as receiving a copy of a test before class).

> **Academic <u>dishonesty</u> includes the following:**
> 1. Registering for a course not approved by a student advisor;
> 2. Unauthorized **copying**, collaboration, or use of notes, books, or other materials on examinations or other academic exercises;
> 3. **Plagiarism**, which is defined as the **intentional** representation of another person's work, words, thoughts, or ideas as one's own;
> 4. **Unauthorized** possession of any academic material, such as tests, research papers, assignments, or similar materials; or
> 5. Furnishing **false** information with the intent to deceive members of the college faculty or administration who are acting in the exercise of their official duties." (durhamtech.edu)

The Student Code of Conduct at Forsyth Tech in Winston Salem, NC includes the following statements:

1. Academic **cheating**, including but not limited to, unauthorized **copying** of academic work of another, collaboration for use of notes or books on examinations **without** prior **permission** of the instructor.

2. Plagiarism or the intentional presentation of work of another **without** proper **acknowledgment** of the source.

3. **Fabrication** and **falsification** or the intentional **misrepresentation** of any information or citation in an academic exercise.

4. Submission of substantial portions of the same academic work for credit more than once without authorization.

5. Abuse of academic materials in the form of destruction, **theft** or **concealment** of library or other resource material or of another student's notes or laboratory experiments.

6. **Complicity** in academic dishonesty in helping or attempting to help another student to commit an act of academic dishonesty.

(http://www.forsythtech.edu/catalog/1011/page/student-code-of-conduct)

Note all the words in BOLD in the above statements. They are all referring to dishonesty. This includes helping someone else! Generally speaking, honesty is an essential quality for every student to possess.

Penalties for **plagiarism** are severe at the college level. At DTCC, in the first incidence, a zero is given on the assignment. On the second offense, a zero can be given for the course. A third offense can mean academic suspension from a program! Most colleges are concerned that allowing students to resubmit work will not teach them the severity of such violations, so there may not be any recourse. There are suggestions for avoiding **plagiarism** in the research appendix.

Be aware! Instructors are quite good at catching cheaters, and many colleges have computer programs to check papers for undocumented material. And while it may seem very generous to help others in "need," the one who abets in plagiarism is also guilty. The best policy is **honesty**—get the help you need, so you can feel proud of the degree you earn and show competency in your career.

Practicum Activity on Plagiarism:

Look at the following scenarios and discuss potential approaches to avoid plagiarism by either party involved:

Scenario 1:

John has been very busy lately with his job and sick child. He has gotten behind in his homework assignments. He asks Susie for help, so she loans him her completed homework to copy.

Scenario 2:

John has not purchased his book for the semester. He needs it to complete his bookwork assignment (which will be graded). He asks Mary to "borrow" her textbook. Mary feels for John's situation, but is afraid to loan her book; therefore, she loans him her completed work.

Scenario 3:

John has a paper due tomorrow, so he goes to the Internet and looks up information for his research. He copies and pastes information into his MS Word document and adds some writing of his own. He does not cite the reference (website) where he got the information, nor does he put the reference in the bibliography.

Reflection: What would you do if you knew one of your classmates is cheating (either during a test or outside of class on other assignments)?

Classroom Etiquette

Etiquette is a term that refers to the behavior appropriate for an event or activity. No one acts the same way around his/her grandmother as his/her buddies or friends. Behavior is important to employers as well. In one survey, some of the personal qualities employers desired included "promptness, respect, responsibility, honesty, sociability, self-management, self-esteem, and basic **etiquette**." (durhamtech.edu)

So what is the etiquette expected of students in the college classroom? First, college is **not** high school, so behaviors tolerated in that setting are not tolerated in a college setting. Here are some things to consider:

1. **Communicate with respect.** This means talking at appropriate times with meaningful language (not slang or vulgar). Students should not attack each other's thoughts or those of the instructor. Students should be sensitive to those of various ethnic or cultural differences.

2. **Act with respect.** Loud or distracting noises such as rattling personal items or food wrappers or cell phone ringing should be avoided during class times. These things distract the student involved as well as his/her neighbors. Turn cell phones off (not vibrate which is still distracting!).

3. **Act with interest.** Nodding and maintaining alert eye contact with the instructor let him/her know you are actively engaged in the learning process. Again, avoid the cell phone texting or computer activity when the instructor is teaching or there is a class activity such as a discussion.

4. **Enter prepared.** Bringing your class materials and tools such as pens, highlighters, calculator, and textbooks will help you learn efficiently and without distractions.

5. **Come healthy.** If you are running a fever or having symptoms that are clearly overwhelming (more than a cold), then stay home and rest. Contact your instructor immediately for assignments and let him/her know you are still part of the class (even if it's the rare absence!). Drink plenty of water (carry a bottle with you), sleep regularly and bring a light jacket or sweater because most colleges are challenged by environmental comfort. Get a flu shot, and both

the hepatitis and meningitis vaccinations since you are in close quarters to many others!

6. **Arrive promptly**. It is even better to arrive slightly early, so you can get out your notes, assignments that are due, and writing instruments (You should sharpen your pencils before class since some colleges don't provide a sharpener in classrooms). Take a moment to relax and focus, so you're revved up for class when it begins.

Most colleges have a student "Code of Conduct" which all students are expected to follow. That code often refers to disruption of the educational process or environment. The majority of those who come to the college campus have come as serious, dedicated students; they desire an environment that allows everyone to learn, so disruptions are not tolerated. Nearly all former high school students remember the class clown, the student who seems to find reasons to disrupt the class or distract the teacher. Colleges are not the place for such behavior, and serious students avoid those who behave so immaturely.

Just remember, etiquette will help you function as a strong student. It shows the instructor you are serious about learning and earning a good grade!

Reflection: Do you remember a time you felt "embarrassed" or angry toward a fellow student whose behavior disrupted a class? Now, think about how you might respond if this happens in your college class.

Communicating Is Important

College is an experience that helps adults grow in many skills, and one of those is communication and self-advocation (speaking up for one's rights or needs). Many times students need to question or clarify important issues in their interactions with instructors. They need to talk to instructors about attendance issues, grade concerns, or even classroom participation or instruction. Students work co-operatively in the classroom which may necessitate some mediation. Here are some tips for improved communication.

What to say:

- Say exactly what you mean. Give details.
- Don't be emotional or bring up the past.
- Ask if the person understands what you've said.

How to say it:

- Calmly. Don't be threatening, whiny, shaky, or sarcastic.
- Use "I feel…" statements rather than "You are…" (Accusing others can make them defensive, and no one can deny your feelings.)

When & where to say it:

- Always be assertive but notice when & where you are (it may not be the right time or place for the other person).
- Do it in private. (Not in front of others-including classmates.)
- Do it when the other person (and you) is not sick, angry or emotional.
- Beware of using e-mail or texting. It is easy to write angry or hurtful thoughts, but it's not easy to undo once you "send" them.

Study Skills Practice: Annotate in the margin about something you should have communicated to an instructor (you can use an example from previous schooling such as high school).

BEING ASSERTIVE

Knowing how to communicate but not communicating will limit your ability to get what you need—whether it is extra instruction or just expressing an opinion. **Assertiveness** is important to your successful communication as a student. You should say what you think, feel and want. You have the right to express yourself.

There are some basic rules for being an assertive communicator. Speak directly, honestly and tactfully without excuses, apologies, or "beating around the bush." Always respect others' rights. Disrespect is disruptive in the educational or work environment and may drive away those who can help you. Consult the list in the first chapter, to find the personnel you need. Finally, assertiveness doesn't mean you should intimidate or manipulate others. The first is considered harassment while the other is considered the ultimate in egocentricity.

Use these tips when communicating with instructors, administrators, and other students!

TIPS:

1. Use confident body language.
   * ★ Look people in the eye.
   * ★ Keep your body straight.
   * ★ Don't point or fidget with things.

2. Be a good listener.
   * ★ Give your full attention to the person talking.
   * ★ Show interest by nodding or saying "yes" or "I understand."
   * ★ Repeat briefly to the person what he or she has said.

3. Respect yourself.
   * ★ Your ideas & feelings are important, even when someone doesn't agree with you.

4. Respect others.
   * ★ Everyone has the right to express feelings & opinions.

What Are Your Attitudes About Education?

What did you feel when you made your decision to get your degree or diploma? Excited? Anxious? Apprehensive? Did any of those feelings slow your decision or make it more urgent?

Your attitude toward school has been shaped by many experiences:

- ❖ childhood schooling
- ❖ parents' educational backgrounds
- ❖ negative experiences in school
- ❖ friends' attitudes toward school
- ❖ peer pressure
- ❖ competing priorities, such as work and family
- ❖ societal views on education

You may or may not be able to pinpoint which experiences or people shaped your attitude; however, any negative feelings you have when it comes to attending class, doing class-work, studying or taking a test, or even succeeding in school may stem from these influences.

Following is a survey you can take which will help you consider any experiences that affect your educational journey.

Remember! Be honest. Take a moment and clear your mind before you begin the survey. Of course, this is just a survey and does not predict all attitude issues.

An Educational Attitude Survey

Rank each situation with a number 1-3 (if it doesn't apply, skip it). Note that the numbers may represent (see words below them) something different in each item:

		1	2	3
1.	My parents finished high school.	both	one	none
2.	My siblings finished high school.	all	some	none
3.	My children must finish or have finished high school.	all	some	none
4.	My children are enrolled in school now.	all	some	none
5.	My children have had trouble in school.	all	some	none
6.	I participate with the PTA.	a lot	some	none
7.	My parents helped me with schoolwork.	a lot	some	none
8.	I have helped my children with schoolwork.	a lot	some	none
9.	I had success in school.	some	a little	none
10.	Teachers always treated me with respect.	most	some	none
11.	Teachers helped me with assignments.	most	some	none
12.	Teachers help my children with assignments.	most	some	none
13.	My parents were proud of my grades in school.	a lot	some	none
14.	My parents encouraged me to stay in school.	a lot	some	none
15.	My friends finished high school.	most	some	none
16.	My coworkers know I do not have a diploma.	most	some	none
17.	My coworkers know I'm taking classes.	most	some	none

18.	My boss is pressuring me to finish school.	1 none	2 some	3 a lot
19.	My family is encouraging me about my classes.	1 a lot	2 some	3 none
20	I look forward to celebrating with friends and family when I graduate.	1 a lot	2 some	3 none
21.	I completed my homework when I was in high school.	1 most	2 some	3 none
22.	A high school diploma was something most in my childhood neighborhood valued.	1 a lot	2 some	3 none
23.	Once I was able to start school, I looked forward to completing my diploma or degree.	1 a lot	2 some	3 none
24.	I have friends who have a college degree.	1 some	2 few	3 none
25.	I plan (or have begun) to go on to college.	1 sure	2 maybe	3 no
26.	I like to read about new ideas.	1 some	2 a bit	3 no
27.	My teachers criticized me in school.	1 no	2 some	3 a lot
28.	I skipped classes when I was in high school.	1 no	2 some	3 a lot
29.	I may skip class or work now.	1 no	2 some	3 a lot
30.	I feel comfortable with my adult instructors.	1 most	2 some	3 none
31.	I ask questions whenever I need to.	1 most	2 some	3 none
32.	I think instructors grade fairly.	1 most	2 some	3 none
33.	I expect my children to do well in school.	1 always	2 some	3 no
34.	Our neighborhood children complete homework.	1 most	2 some	3 no

35.	I like my classmates.	1	2	3
		most	some	no
36.	I enjoy going to class	1	2	3
		most	some	no
37.	I have talked to my children's teachers.	1	2	3
		most	some	no
38.	I have encouraged others to go back to school or enroll in college.	1	2	3
		some	few	none
39.	A diploma or degree is good to have even if it doesn't get someone a better job.	1	2	3
		yes	maybe	no
40.	I grew up in a rural area.	1	2	3
		no	a while	yes
41.	I grew up in an urban area.	1	2	3
		yes	a while	no
42.	I like to teach others about things I know.	1	2	3
		yes	some	no
43.	The best thing about school was recess.	1	2	3
		no	some	yes!
44.	I feel sick during tests.	1	2	3
		no	some	yes!
45.	I looked forward to getting my grade reports.	1	2	3
		most	some	no
46.	I can't wait for the next break or holiday.	1	2	3
		a bit	some	no
47.	I usually get my homework done.	1	2	3
		most	some	no
48.	I'd rather do housework or chores than homework.	1	2	3
		no	sometimes	yes
49.	Sitting still in class is difficult.	1	2	3
		no	sometimes	yes
50.	I know exactly what time it is without looking.	1	2	3
		no	sometimes	yes

Total each column & add all 3 numbers: _____ + _____ + _____ = _____

Did you feel strange or anxious while you took the survey? This may even be a clue to your attitudes toward education.

Please remember this was not meant to make you feel bad about your attitude. Actually, it must be already good since you have enrolled in this course! The survey is meant to help you explore why you might feel anxious or upset at times when you are in class, doing homework, or taking tests.

When you have these anxious feelings, stop for a moment and THINK. You'll remember some of the good and bad influences you've had!
Now the results:

1	-	50	great attitude
51	-	75	good attitude most of time
76	-	109	some anxiety
110	-	150	can be very anxious

> **Reflection**: In the margin, list some **good** influences or experiences you've had either in school or about school.

Use the list to change any attitudes if needed! You may seek help from your instructor, fellow classmates or even the college's counseling service. Set goals to change one attitude at a time; you may find that one attitude change will lead to another and another. A positive, hard-working attitude is expected in our society and work world, so college is the right place to begin adding the best attitudes!

Have a Positive Attitude!

Attitudes can change everything. We shape our own attitudes even when it seems justified to be upset or annoyed. In the educational setting, attitude can affect the student's grade, success in a program, and interactions with classmates, school administration and instructors. Napoleon Hill, author and motivational speaker, points out in his writing, that a positive attitude in the employment arena is essential because it affects who's likely to get promoted, who becomes part of the leadership and whose output is most productive. He also points out that a positive attitude will reduce stress and its negative impact on a person's health. (http://www.positive-attitude-tips.com) Here are some additional tips to help you remain positive as a student:

☐ It's okay to make mistakes.
☐ Say to yourself: "I'd like to be good at this but if I'm not, that's okay.
☐ Asking questions is never stupid.
☐ I can say "No" when I need to.
☐ Just because I see that way, others may not, and they don't have to see it my way.
☐ I can stand up for myself and say what I feel.
☐ Everyone's feelings are his/her own.

Reflection. Think about something you have a negative feeling about. Write about how you can make that negative attitude a positive one.

Setting Goals

Setting goals will help you focus on plans in your life. Goals give you direction and aim!

Activity 1. Brainstorm everything you would like to do. Be concrete and be visionary! No goal is too wild.

❖Activity 2. Categorize your goals into the following timetables.

1 Month	**1 Semester**	**1 year**
_____	_____	_____
_____	_____	_____
_____	_____	_____
_____	_____	_____
_____	_____	_____
_____	_____	_____
_____	_____	_____

❖ Activity 3. Take your 1-month list, and divide it into weekly plans. Include the steps you'll need to take in order to accomplish the goals.

Week 1	Week 2	Week 3	Week 4
_____	_____	_____	_____
_____	_____	_____	_____
_____	_____	_____	_____

❖ **Interactive Sharing.** Discuss with a partner how you will accomplish one of your one-year goals.

SMART Goal Setting

As you decide what you want to accomplish academically and professionally, ask yourself if your goals are SMART.

Specific	You are more likely to achieve a specific goal than a general goal. When you write your goals, consider the five Ws: who, what, where, when, and why.
Measurable	Establish a way to determine whether or not you achieve your goals. When you can measure your goals, you can figure out how well you are progressing and adapt when necessary.
Attainable	Choose goals that you can achieve. If your goals are attainable, then you are more likely to achieve them. Set yourself up for success rather than failure.
Realistic	To reach your goals, you must be *willing* and *able* to do the work that your goals require. If your goal is to earn a 4.0 GPA, but you aren't *willing* to dedicate the time necessary to study for your classes, then you have established an unrealistic goal.
Time-Bound	Establish a deadline, so you can know when to evaluate whether or not you have achieved your goal and to create a sense of urgency.

Look at the examples below to see how to change vague goals into SMART goals.

Vague Example #1: I will lose weight.
SMART Revision: I will lose 10 pounds in six months by limiting sweets and exercising every week.

This goal is specific and measurable (*lose 10 pounds*), attainable and time bound (*six months allowed*), and realistic (*limiting sweets and exercising weekly is doable for most people*).

Vague Example #2: I will pass my classes.
SMART Revision: I will earn a B in BIO 111 and an A in ENG 111 this semester.

This goal is specific and measurable (*naming the exact grades and the exact classes*), attainable (*students can earn these grades*), and time bound (*at the end of the semester, you will find out these grades*). The only criterion that is questionable is whether or not the goal is realistic. If this student is willing and able to do the work required to earn these grades, then it is realistic. If the student is unwilling or unable to do the work required, then it is not realistic.

So as you set goals, you should evaluate them. Look at the following for a chart that will help you determine how 'SMART' your goals are.

Evaluating Goals Practice

Directions: Read the goals listed below and put a check mark under S, M, A, R, and/or T if the goal is **S**pecific, **M**easurable, **A**ttainable, **R**ealistic, and/or **T**ime-bound. If any of the elements are missing, re-write the goal to make it SMART.

Goal	S	M	A	R	T
1. I will improve my time management this semester. *Revision*: I will use a weekly planner to keep up with assignments and activities this semester.			✓	✓	✓
2. I will make a good grade in this class. *Revision*:					
3. I will graduate with an Associate's degree in one year. *Revision*:					
4. I will be successful. *Revision*:					
5. I will spend at least one hour studying for psychology every Tuesday evening this semester. *Revision*:					
6. I will start my own business in the next 10 years. *Revision*:					

Now try setting your personal SMART goals with the activity on the next page.

My SMART GOALS!

Directions: Write one academic goal and one professional goal in the table below. Put a check mark under S, M, A, R, and/or T if the goal is **S**pecific, **M**easurable, **A**ttainable, **R**ealistic, and/or **T**ime-bound. If any of the elements are missing, re-write the goal to make it SMART.

Goal	S	M	A	R	T

Long-Term Goal Setting

The previous activities were based on short-term goal setting. These may need revising on a weekly or monthly basis. We also need long-term goals. These become life goals and are shaped by our need for relationships, beliefs, and accomplishments as we grow older.

Activity 5: Write down three of your five-year goals.

Reflection writing: Where would you like to be in 10 years? 20 years? How will education play a part?

Application: Write your goals on a sheet of paper and put it where you can find it in a year or five years or ten years. On your birthday or New Year's, go back and look at them. Are you on track? How have they've been modified? Take courage—sometimes, we're only delayed in accomplishing goals. Also, we may change them because of family or career or life events. Always remember, you can still reach them! Aim for the stars! Use the Mind Map on the next page for planning long-term goals. Break up your long-term goals into short-term steps. This will help you focus on your long-term goals more regularly. Don't forget to make your goals **SMART**!

Reflection:

1. Do you have a goal for each semester?

2. What are potential obstacles you face in each semester?

3. How do you plan to overcome obstacles you might face?

Goal

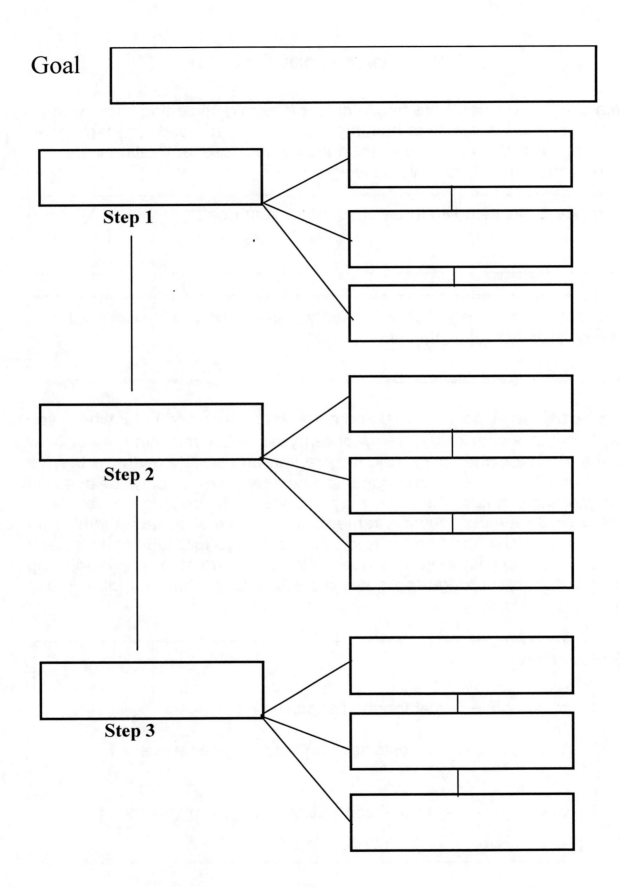

Step 1

Step 2

Step 3

Career Goals

Susie remembers how she used to stare up at the sky and wonder what the stars were composed of or how they moved (or appeared to) through the heavens. She wondered what it was like to actually walk on the moon, just as she had seen Armstrong do that fateful night. She dreamed of leaving her footprints on some distant planet.

As Susie grew up, she took classes such as physics and chemistry in order to prepare for her university studies. She read books on flying to the stars; Asimov and Einstein were her mentors. She worked hard in math and took extra classes to prepare to go to college.

When Susie applied to the University of North Carolina, she wrote an essay about how she wanted to study the stars and how the universe impacted everyone on the planet Earth. Pouring over the university catalogue, she marked every physics course. She wanted to take them all!

What Susie began to realize as she entered her second year of college is that she had not really planned on a career. Would she be a physicist? Would she be an astronomer? Could she enter the Air Force and become an astronaut? She had not considered the military.

Susie needed a career plan. She would talk to her faculty advisor and learn that to become a physicist she would need to obtain a Ph.D. in the field. Astronomers were not in great demand and also required extensive education. She would need to look at the college's ROTC program to enter the military. That would mean more classes. After many discussions, review of her grades, and setting long and short-term goals, Susie would make a decision.

So what is your career goal? Have you looked at your life's goals? Are you prepared to go the "extra mile" for education? Do you have the support of your family for such a journey? Will you be satisfied with the work you choose? Following is a page of career considerations. Spend some time looking at your goals and researching your career. Then you can make your plans!

Career Goal Exploration

My Career goal is			
Skills Necessary for Career			
Benefits of career			
Salary range			
Where I can work (Geographical)			

Educational needs		College That Offers	Time to complete
	Certificate		
	Diploma		
	Associates		
	Bachelors		
	Masters		
	Apprenticeship		
	Military experience		

Internship Time and place
Advancement Possibilities
Career future (will it be needed?)
Other considerations such as family and spouse/mate's career

Places to research: Occupational Outlook Handbook (www.bls.gov) or College Foundation sites such as www.cfnc.org.

I AM--I CAN!   MY STRENGTHS

Adults bring a myriad of qualities, strengths, and experiences to their educational experiences. Sometimes, however, they do not know how (or that they should) to tap those strengths and experiences. Think about those qualities that make you who you are.

Now list six words or phrases that tell the most about you and then write down how you can use those qualities in your education.

EXAMPLE: I am laid back; there fore, I get along with others well.

I am…	therefore I can…

Now that you have listed your strengths, think about how they affect the goals you have set for yourself. There are a number of websites that help assess your strengths or preference, such as the Holland Codes. These self assessments will help you understand (or decide) the path you've chosen for yourself with your education or training.

The Undecided Student

What if I haven't decided on a definite career? Many students enter college and don't have their career futures clearly decided (or refined). First, remember that a college degree is a strong indicator to any employer that you are persistent, forward-thinking and trainable. A general education associate's degree can be used as a stepping stone in career advancement or future education.

Other students come to the community college to get training quickly in a temporary or "stop-over" career that will support them and their families until they do decide on a final career goal.

A third category of students are those who attend college because it's expected of them. Parents may "persuade" the student that it's the right thing to do, even though he or she hasn't made a final decision on a direction. Many of us did not know at 18 what we would be doing at 40. Some of us are still searching for that perfect career point.

So what should you do if you're undecided? Use the stages of goal discernment to help you. First, try some of the self-assessments in this book, such as the Myer-Briggs or Holland Codes, to see if you can at least move in a general direction of a career area. For instance, a student like Tamara is interested in a medical field such as being a physician or nurse or researcher, but for now she plans to major in biology at the university. She should start with the University Transfer program at a local community college and perhaps even do the short course for EMS level one and do a volunteer stint with the local EMS service.

Also, take time for career exploration. Research is key here. Go to websites such as the *Occupational Outlook Handbook* at www.bls.gov/oco and read about possible career areas. Ask someone about job shadowing where you can observe the career in action. Interview faculty at the community college about career areas that are related to the courses they teach. Keep your notes and research handy, so you can continue in your goal setting and values development. Finally, don't worry if you find your career path in motion; many adults find their interests and needs changing as they progress in their life-span development. As a college student, you have a wide world of possibilities.

PRIORITIES

What are your priorities? What are the activities that you choose to schedule and how do these affect your day or week? Often we are faced with choices both in the roles we play and the activities we must complete on a day-to-day basis.

Some activities are urgent (must be taken care of now) while others are not urgent (can be done later). Additionally, some activities are important and others are unimportant. Some are urgent and important while others are neither urgent nor important. Look at the following list and place each in the grid on the following page.

- ❖ Death of a loved one
- ❖ Child has a slight earache
- ❖ Taking your friend/child to the mall
- ❖ Light bill due in ten days
- ❖ Paper due at the end of the semester/mini-session
- ❖ Walking the dog
- ❖ Test on three chapters in math tomorrow
- ❖ Favorite show on television tonight

- ❖ Clean out the fridge
- ❖ Dog needs shots
- ❖ Phone call from a friend
- ❖ Grocery shopping
- ❖ Reading junk mail
- ❖ Trip to library for a class project
- ❖ Birthday party
- ❖ Text message on cell phone
- ❖ Recertification for food stamps
- ❖ FAFSA deadline in two weeks

After you've completed your placement of these activities, reconsider the placements. Is each in an appropriate priority? We may consider things like a phone call as urgent; however, if it's just chit-chat, the call is not urgent or important. Use the following chart for your own activities. Examine carefully where you place each. Don't be afraid to rearrange your priorities!

Life Management

	URGENT	NOT URGENT
IMPORTANT		
NOT IMPORTANT		

	URGENT	NOT URGENT
IMPORTANT		
NOT IMPORTANT		

Reflection Writing: Is there an activity you need to complete this week that is both urgent and important? How will you accomplish it?

A Prioritizing Technique

When using a "to-do" list, it is best to stop for a moment and consider the priority of each item on the list. Several time management and success program use an alphabetizing method. In *Eat That Frog*, by Brian Tracy (2001), a five step priority system is suggested. It includes the following:

1. Assign an "A" to all top-priority items. These are tasks that must be done within a set timeframe. If there is more than one, then add a 1, 2, 3, etc. among the A-items.

2. Assign a "B" to things that need to be done, but the completion is not timebound.

3. Assign a "C" for things you'd like to get done, but they are not necessary to complete current goals—these could be those personal tasks such as household chores.

4. Assign a "D" to tasks you could get someone else to do— know as delegation; perhaps this is a roommate or classmate. Remember, you don't have to do EVERYTHING yourself to be successful.

5. Finally, give an "E" to all the rest of the items. These really become your elimination tasks. You may have thought you had to do these tasks, like calling your friends everyday; however, in reality, they are time wasters.

Brian Tracy's book is great read to help anyone avoid procrastinating, since this is the goal of a good time manager. This (or any similar method) will keep you less stressed and more focused on accomplishing your program studies.

STUDY SKILL PRACTICE:

Highlight the action words in the previous pages on time management. Then list in the margin, two methods you will try NOW. Remember, procrastination is the student's archenemy!

Graduation Notes!

One of your goals should be graduation, so here are some inspiring words written by those who have gone before you!

Graduation
Rejoicing, happy
Amazing, exciting, fun
Diploma
Unite
An outstanding day
Tears of happiness
End   --CS, 1995

Gaining control over life,
Running for a harder life
Around and around
Deciding decisions
Understanding life's expectations
Against a man
That shakes your hand…
Exciting new beginnings! --CB, 1995

Great
Real hard work
Academic
Diploma
U did it!!
All over now!!!
Tassel
Excited   --GT, 1995

Gloat
Rapture
Arrangement
Delightful
Uplifting
Anxious
Turning Point
Eagerness --anonymous AHSD student

Make up your own acrostic sentence or acronym about graduation:

G
R
A
D
U
A
T
E

Final Words About Success

I can give you a six-word formula for success: "Think things through--then follow through."   --Edward Rickenbacker

Making a success of the job at hand is the best step toward the kind you want. --Bernard M. Baruch

Always bear in mind that your own resolution to succeed is more important than any one thing. --Abraham Lincoln

---

"Be decisive: …the Obama Way…Everybody speaks his or her mind…then Barack makes the decision. After that, there is absolutely no second-guessing or looking back…The trick is to stick with it…It's better to have one strategy and stick to it…than to try ten in pursuit of the perfect answer. The point is that there is no perfect answer." (Interview from www.msnbc.msn.com)

Make up your own…

_____

_____

_____

            --A saying by _____.
                     (your name)

Scenarios and Practicum

Read each scenario and think of suggestions to redirect or improve the student's concerns.

1. Jonathan has decided to return to college after a ten-year break (due to family and need to work). His wife is concerned that he will become too anxious or become overwhelmed and not persevere. What can help Jonathan become more determined?

2. Sue has decided to return to school to become a nurse after working as a CNA for 20 years. Her three children are still in high school and often have demands on her time and energy. How can she stay focused?

3. John had difficulty finishing high school last spring, but he wants to pursue a career in computer programming. His parents have expected him to go to the university and get a Bachelor's degree. The local community college offers an Associates in Applied Science. How can John convince his parents that this is the correct educational path for him?

4. Sara has to work full-time and attend college at night and on weekends. It will take her two extra years to complete her Associate's degree. How can Sara stay encouraged?

5. Fred has dropped out of college twice. He has decided that if he doesn't succeed this semester, he will not try again. How can Fred persist and be successful (besides studying hard)?

What the Students Say...

There are times that my academic life can get hard. There are times I don't want to go to school..but communication helps me to get back up and go to school. FJ (2008)

My favorite time of day to do homework is early afternoon and late night..because if I do it in early afternoon, I can go back and review later that night. NG (2008)

In my opinion the most important attribute a student can have is a positive attitude. MS (2008)

Being on time shows your teacher you care about what goes on in class and what kind of work you turn in...BJ (2008)

Chapter 3
Organization for
the Successful
Student

Notebooks
Computers
Calendar Use
Time Management
Study Times
Decision Making
Learning Styles
Files

An Introduction to Getting Organized

As an adult, as well as a student, organization is the key to life management. There are many aspects to this including time management, materials arrangement, and decision making. To get started, make sure you have the tools you need for the job you are about to undertake. You should get these by your first day of class to assure you won't get behind or be unprepared for class. Here is a suggested list:

- ☐ Pens (colors that are easy for you to read and a type you enjoy using)
- ☐ Pencils (mechanical is best)
- ☐ 1-or 2-inch 3-ring binder (one for each class)—excellent to put handouts in and to easy remove and manipulate your class notes!
- ☐ Dividers for notebooks
- ☐ Lab notebooks for science classes
- ☐ Sticky notes
- ☐ Highlighters (yellow)
- ☐ USB (flash/thumb) drive
- ☐ Collegiate dictionary (electronic also nice)
- ☐ Thesaurus
- ☐ Water bottle
- ☐ Book bag or messenger bag—comfortable to carry
- ☐ Covers for rental textbooks
- ☐ Textbooks!

While your college bookstore carries many of these items, you can save money by going to a discount store such as Wal-Mart or a dollar store. Textbook costs are often higher than your tuition and fees at a community college, so look for signs posted by other students who are selling their textbooks. Go online and look for copies of your texts; most can ship within a couple of days of ordering, and even with delivery cost, you may save significantly. Check the college bookstore's website or on-site location to get the names of the books you'll need. ALWAYS double check the edition number (these are essential) and/or get the ISBN number to order from another source. If you can do this before the semester begins, then do so; otherwise, check your college library for copies on reserve (ones that can be used in the library only) to do assignments and stay current. If you are waiting on financial aid, instructors do not accept this as an excuse for not doing work or having books for class, so be creative by finding alternative sources to purchase your texts!

Organizing Your Notebook

A three-ring notebook (not a spiral!) is essential to help you organize your notes, homework and project assignments, and necessary course handouts. In some classes, the entire course may consist of paper handouts; additionally, many students want the hardcopies of electronic files, although electronic, online materials are the future and reduce the students' carbon footprint! The papers you collect in your notebook also may be graded at the **end** of a course. This kind of organization is important in the work/career world as well since not every environment is electronically based; for instance, businesses have to give paper receipts or customer information (such as a car repair or patient diagnosis), so paper copies must be organized. Many instructors still require students to hand in paper copies, and those graded papers should be kept until a final course grade is submitted (and checked or confirmed by the student). A notebook also protects your assignments; never be the student who shows up in class and declares, "I dropped my homework assignment in the mud on the way to class today!" (Actual student excuse!)

Finally, the tests for your organized notebook are twofold: **1.** Hold up your notebook (open side down) and shake it. Nothing should fall out. **2.** Find an important document such as your syllabus, today's homework or a semester project in 10 seconds. If you can do both, your notebook is on the way to being organized!

Use these strategies to organize each of your course notebooks:

- Organize your notebooks with LABELED TABS!
    - Contents of your notebook:

        - Section 1 … Calendar and Syllabus
        - Section 2… Class Notes/Activities/handouts
        - Section 3… Projects
        - Section 4… Quizzes and Study Guides
        - Section 5… Homework

- KEEP all your work until you have a final grade. (*continued on next page…*)

- ALWAYS carry your notebook with you. You should never arrive notebookless—it's like being swordless in a battle!
- DATE all handouts and note pages.
- USE your planner.
  - Go over each syllabus and all paper or project sheets, and write in your planner what is due when.
  - Put other classes' due dates as well, so you can get a "big picture" of the things you're doing.
  - Put important appointments and work hours in it.
- PUNCH holes in any handouts that don't have them.

OKADUP! OK it ADds UP!

Reflection: How have you used notebooks in the past? Why is a spiral notebook ineffective?

Students and Computer Use

While it is NOT vital you own a computer, every student should have regular access to one. Most colleges have open computer labs where students can do work. Your college may provide students with e-mail accounts which they must activate; this is where the college and instructors will send vital alerts such as when to preregister for a new semester or class cancellations or changes. If your college does not provide an e-mail account, get one (see below) that is just for your college needs (Name it *college—your name; example: DTCC-janicestuart@____*).

Your USB drive (see Appendix) will be your prime storage device, so you can carry your work back and forth safely. Be sure to save your work on your drive since most labs delete all work saved on the computers there every night. Save work in a Rich Text Format (rtf) document, so you can open word-processing documents at any computer with any word-processing program. If you don't know much about computers or don't feel comfortable using them, take an introductory computer course your first semester.

E-mail is an important form of communication using the computer and Internet. College instructors often REQUIRE that students have e-mail addresses, so they can communicate important information. You can also e-mail yourself research and important document (for instance, if you need to print it out at another physical site. Follow the instructions below to set up an e-mail account.

<u>**Setting Up E-mail Instructions**</u>:

✓ www.gmail.com
✓ www.yahoo.com
✓ www.hotmail.com

1.   Open your Internet Browser.
2.   Type in one of these addresses:
3.   Click on **Sign-up**!
4.   Fill in all the information required in the boxes.
5.   Read over the Terms of Agreement and click on **I accept**.
6.   Write down your e-mail address and password!
7.   Type in your e-mail address, login name, and password and click **OK**.
   You now have an e-mail account and can send e-mail.

Most colleges have what is known as a "learning management system" such as Blackboard or Moodle. If your instructor has your class (or some of it) loaded online, take time as soon as possible to go to that site and explore its contents. Click on the links to various content items such as the syllabus or course outline. Look for assignments. Electronic copies can be very useful for project completion since they often provide items where you can enter information in a required form (such as a diagram or table). The LMS can also let you have access to your course even when you've left book or notebook in a different physical place than where you are currently, wondering what assignment you think is due (while trying to plan whether you've got something else pressing to do rather than socialize or work extra hours). Finally, instructors may post assignments online that must be done in that format. Watch out for deadlines; some tests or assignments may "disappear" or end at a required time. So if that test must be done by midnight on Monday, don't wait until 11:50 to begin; it will stop working at the designated time.

The Internet has opened our learning world into one giant classroom and library resource. Students should still very cautious about which websites to use in order to help them complete assignments. This is a very easy, tempting way to plagiarize information. There is also a lot of misleading information on the Internet, so always use reliable sources such as links provided by your instructor or college library (which provides many educational databases to use). Also, be aware that what you post online at Facebook or other social sites can harm your future. This is a way to get into awkward situations where you need to explain skipping class or doing other questionable activities (such as underage partying). Future employers also check these websites which may reveal your personal ethics or point of view that conflicts with the employers'.

One final word, CAUTION! Don't use your computer as a time-waster. It is easy to waste time on the Internet or gaming or chatting with friends. Schedule these times just like you would any activity.

Using a Planner

You may already be using a calendar to mark important days like holidays, birthdays, and vacations. Most adults use calendars to keep track of appointments, pay days, special school events, bill due dates and other important need-to-know dates. Yet, have you ever thought about using a weekly **planner** to succeed in your educational pursuits?

Most instructors have a **syllabus**, a list or schedule of lessons to be covered and tests to be given, but some of these do not have a definite time table. You can use your planner several ways to augment your class syllabus:

1> Ask your instructor to give you a time table (even if it's only two or three weeks at a time). Mark these in your planner.

2> Divide up the reading and work assignments, so that your studying is more evenly paced before a test. Remember to leave a few days to study before your test dates! In a self-study class, you set your own time table for tests and lessons to cover.

3> Online or hybrid courses usually have a schedule of set dates (and perhaps exact hours) to submit work. Once the time has passed, you may not be able to turn in work. Make sure you are very comfortable with submitting work electronically. Deadlines often move by too quickly to be inefficient with the computer.

Remember to put ALL your dates and appointments in the planner, then you can get a good idea of what your study schedule looks like. Check your calendar often and check off completed tasks. Finally, don't be afraid to adjust your schedule as you need to. A day of doctor appointments or work may conflict with a test date, so you may need to adjust your appointments or ask your instructor (well in advance!) to reschedule your test dates. Purchase a student planner at your college bookstore or use a PDA that beeps.

> **Application:** Go through your textbook or syllabus and mark down the pages you will do to prepare for tests on your calendar.

Some Tips on Time Management

Time management begins with a calendar, but that's only the BIG picture. Adults live on a day-to-day basis, so a daily schedule should be mapped out. Of course, these schedules can change from week to week, although most schedules are steady for a few weeks or months--such as your college semester.

Why are schedules important? They help adults get things done on time and complete goals. A schedule can even provide leisure time.

If you've never written your schedule down, you may be surprised how much you do or how much time you may actually have to get things done. Use the schedule in Appendix D and block out the activities you do on a daily basis. Use the following checklist to make sure your schedule is complete:

___ 1. Wake up time/breakfast/getting ready
___ 2. Travel time to and from work or school
___ 3. Class and lab times
___ 4. Employment schedule
___ 5. Chore time
___ 6. Meal preparation and eating
___ 7. Special times with children (playtime, bath-time, homework)
___ 8. Religious observations
___ 9. Down time or relaxation/ sleep period
___ 10. Study (Plan at least two hours outside of class for every hour in class.)

Don't worry if you can't keep completely on schedule since this should only be a guide. Later in this section are some tips on "Studying with just a little bit of time."

Re-Evaluation: Copy the following schedule and do an analysis. On one copy, write down what you SPECULATE you will do over the next week. On a second copy, RECORD the ACTUAL week's activities. Then compare the two by looking at these questions:
- o What surprised you about your time use?
- o What activities were your greatest "time-wasters"?
- o What activities did you put off (procrastinated)?
- o What can you do better? What can you eliminate or combine?

Weekly Time Analysis Worksheet

DO THIS GRID TWICE! The first time, **SPECULATE** what you plan to do; second time, what you ACTUALLY did.

	Monday	Tuesday	Wednesday	Thursday	Friday	Saturday	Sunday
midnight							
1:00 a.m.							
2:00 a.m.							
3:00 a.m.							
4:00 a.m.							
5:00 a.m.							
6:00 a.m.							
7:00 a.m.							
8:00 a.m.							
9:00 a.m.							
10:00 am							
11:00 am							
noon							
1:00 p.m.							
2:00 p.m.							
3:00 p.m.							
4:00 p.m.							
5:00 p.m.							
6:00 p.m.							
7:00 p.m.							
8:00 p.m.							
9:00 p.m.							
10:00 p.m.							
11:00 p.m.							

Permission to photocopy/additional copy in Appendix D.

Things to Do, Places to Go, People to See

Is your day filled with many (too many) things to do? You may want to consider writing a daily to-do list. Keep a list that you check off. Make sure you aren't filling your list with too many things so that your day is spent rushing from one event to another.

Don't forget your priorities. As a student, you will have the daily tasks to complete assignments and attend class. If your lists are impossible to complete, you should reconsider the list and look at ways to divide the tasks up or get help with completing them.

Reflection/ Activity:

Where do you put your list? Decide where the best location is to look at your list of reminders.

List places you spend time (also list the tools/bags /vehicles you use):

Morning:
Afternoon:
Evening:

Don't like to write things down? This can be a sure way to forget things or neglect your priorities. One last thing: don't over-do the to-do lists. Assignment lists are essential, and make a list of the "big" tasks or chores you must complete. See the sample in Appendix D.

Your Study Time

Now that you have an idea of your daily schedule, you can begin to schedule time for studying. But how much time should you schedule? Some colleges require a minimum of two hours of outside study time for every one hour of class time. For your current courses, you may not need so much time; however, the time you need depends on the assignments you must complete or tests you must study for.

Whatever time you need, it does not always require long chunks of time to have study time. Even small amounts of time can be useful. In any case, you should schedule time, and any time you don't use becomes bonus time.

RE-EVALUATE: Go back and look at your daily schedule and **draw boxes around the time you could study**. If there is no time at all, reconsider things such as free time or other activities that can be shortened or moved. Also, look at times you are doing things that do not require your complete attention, such as doing the laundry or child's naptime, when you can study at the same time. Don't overlook small periods of time 30 minutes or less!

Research shows that using the memory strategy known as distributed practice helps with long-term memory and learning. Distributed practice is studying for short amounts of time (30-60 minutes) over a long period of time (at least two weeks). Use the strategies below to make the most of the distributed practice memory principle. Notice that this concept is the opposite of cramming, which is ineffective in helping you learn subjects long term.

1. Memorize facts during commercials or other "dead time" when you're doing nothing important.

2. Keep note-cards by the sofa or chair you frequent.

3. Use magnets to put copies of your study notes on the refrigerator, or clip them to the visor of your car.

2. Read a few pages at a time. One or two pages or until the end of a section are tasks accomplished in short time periods. Try the 15-5 method where you read or study for 15 minutes then take a 5 minute

break. Don't forget to take a few minutes to think about what you've read or studied. Doing this over a period of weeks results in a cumulative effect—you will have studied for hours before a test!

4. Reviewing notes and highlighting parts of books take only a few minutes. You could do these while waiting for class to start or while you are riding back and forth on a bus.

5. You can do a few math problems or one or two essay questions in a few minutes.

6. Use a checklist to note completed assignments. (See appendix sample)

7. Break up projects into smaller parts. Use your project instruction sheet or **rubric** (a grade-sheet checklist) to make sure you're done!

Of course, you must be organized enough to carry your books and notebooks wherever you go. Think of it as a "badge of honor" to look like the student you are.

When you're done, reward yourself for large tasks completed (entire chapters, essays & papers completed, tests finished).

A Time Management Survey

INSTRUCTIONS: Mark the rating that describes how you feel or think about each statement about using your time.

	STATEMENT	ALWAYS	SOMETIMES	NEVER
1.	I prioritize the tasks I must get done daily.			
2.	I feel stressed when I have a big task.			
3.	I get more little jobs done than bigger ones.			
4.	I write assignments down.			
5.	I get plenty of sleep every day.			
6.	I spend more than 30 minutes relaxing daily.			
7.	I get to do things I **want** to do, not just things I **have** to do.			
8.	I feel relieved when I complete a project.			
9.	I have more things to do than I have time for.			
10.	I have put my family life or social life on hold.			
11.	I complete tasks that are beneficial to my career.			
12.	I never ask others to do things for me.			
13.	I have to redo tasks that I have completed.			
14.	I check my email more than twice a day.			
15.	I surf the Internet every day.			
16.	I often get diverted to busywork tasks.			
17.	I start another task before I finish the one I'm working on.			
18.	I do two or more activities at once.			
19.	I spend every day the way I plan it or want it to go.			
20.	I feel like I'm always trying to catch up.			
21.	I am regularly late for activities or class.			
22.	I can get to the end of the day and not feel like I accomplished much.			
23.	I put off tasks I don't enjoy or like to do.			
24.	I often have urgent things to do.			
25.	My life is organized; I know where important things are.			

Procrastinator or Multi-tasker?

Are you a procrastinator or do you consider yourself to be a multi-tasker? Do you know that the two are actually connected? The connection is actually quite simple; someone who multi-tasks is not really doing any one activity well, and this means s/he is actually putting off (or procrastinating) a task's completion. You may likely see yourself in the same situation as many; you are on the phone, listening to music or watching television, working on the computer and/or trying to complete an assignment for an upcoming class. While you may think you're doing multiple things, your brain is actually only partially processing one or two of these activities. The most important job is getting little concentrated effort.

A number of studies have been done on the multi-tasker and concentration; in fact, psychologists have been studying this phenomenon since the 1890s! (http://chronicle.com/article, February 2010) Clifford Nass of Stanford University reported in this article that, "Heavy multitaskers are often extremely confident in their abilities...but there's evidence that those people are actually worse at multitasking than most people." (http://chronicle.com/article, February 2010) His study concluded that overall, multi-taskers did not do well on memory tasks. That means a student cannot effectively remember details from reading or recall facts or skill-steps for completing problem sets in math, science or writing. In an article published by the *Tampa Tribune*, John Reiners reported that studies reveal that the human brain is actually "hard-wired to do one task at a time." (http://www2.hernandotoday.com/content) He also put it in a more colorful way, "If you chase two rabbits, both will get away." (http://www2.hernandotoday.com) This means productivity is lost!

So, if you don't claim to be a multi-tasker, are you willing to admit to being a procrastinator? It is almost every adult's bane to put off unpleasant tasks such as household chores, or doctor visits, or oil changes. Even if you've committed yourself to being a student and completing your studies, you may find studying outside of class (known as "homework") an activity you often put off until the pressure is on which, of course, leads to stress. So as one author, Brian Tracy, has put it, just gulp it down or eat the frog we hate to face (*Eat That Frog,* 2001)

Why Homework?

Homework may seem like a childish word. It's what the third grade teacher gave you to keep you busy. As an adult learner, you should view homework in a different way. Your attitude may be the root of your procrastinating! Look at the following survey, and check the statements you believe reflect what you think about homework. Be honest!

☐ Homework is busy work.
☐ Homework takes too much of my free time.
☐ Homework should not be assigned on weekends.
☐ Homework is too difficult to do at home.
☐ Instructors should let me do homework in class.
☐ Homework doesn't teach me anything.
☐ I do homework as fast as I can, not worrying about the answers.
☐ I have to read the pages over and over, so I don't like to do homework.
☐ Homework doesn't affect my grades anyway.
☐ Homework can be turned in anytime.
☐ Homework should be gone over every day.
☐ I've used excuses for not turning in my homework on time.
☐ Homework is only for kids.
☐ It's okay to copy someone else's homework.
☐ It's okay to work together on homework.
☐ I do homework while I watch television or talk on the phone.
☐ I do homework on my job.
☐ Family is more important than homework.

Think about your choices. Will these attitudes help or hinder your success? Remember, all aspects of learning can help you reach your goal. If your homework attitude is not the best, decide what you can do help it become a better one.

Reflection. Write down what you will do to improve your attitude or approach to homework or "out-of-class" assignments.

Presentation of Materials

As a student, you are "earning a grade," that is being paid for the work you complete. In business, an employee has certain responsibilities and expectations to meet. When he or she prepares a report or other documents, he or she must present it in proper form. Similar expectations are required of students in the classroom setting.

Check your homework, class work and research papers for the following guidelines:

- ✓ **Neatness.** Typed or written neatly in dark ink (when allowed). Essays/papers should be double-spaced (lines skipped/size 12 font).
- ✓ **Proper Labeling should include:**

  - ✓ Your Name
  - ✓ Date
  - ✓ Chapter number, page number and exercise number

- ✓ **Stapled or clipped together**
- ✓ **Proofread for mistakes**

Instructors reward the special attention given to work. Messier papers can earn lower grades. **Keep all** rough drafts and returned papers **until the end of your semester** and your grade is finalized. Always strive for the business of excellence!

Tip: If your instructor posts questions or assignments online, you can open them up and copy them into your word processor. Then type in your answers. Don't forget to e-mail yourself a copy just in case the hard copy you print doesn't make it to campus.

Files and Staying Organized

When all is said and done for a semester, what should you do with all that work? First, make sure you've gotten the grade you've expected; if you need to talk to the instructor about it, you'll need your notebook with your completed, graded work and tests in it to prove your point.

Next, buy an inexpensive (used at a used office supply store) metal file cabinet to store your notebooks (for at least one year). If you have classes that prepare you for licensure tests, save all notebooks until you've completed and passed these tests! Keep any books that can help you prepare.

Keep records in file folders of your registration history, transcripts, receipts (Tuition and fees are tax-deductible!) and financial aid papers. Put these in one of your file cabinet's drawers.

Keep the work on your USB drive or on a portable zip-drive. You may need to access these later as well. See the appendix on computer use for alternative storage sites for your computer-based work.

While this may seem excessive, it will give you a single place for your work history that you can carry with you or store in a family member's or friend's closet. This history is important as you establish yourself in your career area!

Reflection: How organized do you consider yourself? Can you place your hands on important papers such as bill or credit-card info or your birth certificate? Do you know where your tax returns are and your financial aid papers? If not, do some reorganizing now!

MAKING DECISIONS

As an adult student, you will face many decisions that affect or "repair" issues you face as you pursue your education. These may include job schedules, child-care, financial needs or transportation. Use the following steps to make, put into action and evaluate.

Step 1:   Define the problem. Be exact. Ask "What CAUSES this problem?"

Step 2:   Gather Information. Set aside some time to work on the problem. Brainstorm all possibilities. Seek advice. Take notes. Use all your resources.

Step 3:   Write down your goals and priorities that must be met to solve the problem. List your pros & cons. Choose the best solution.

Step 4:   Put your plan into ACTION!

Step 5:   Reevaluate your problem and solution plan. Are your plans working? Are you on schedule? (Remember: Don't delay!)

Step 6:   Follow-up. Did it work? Is there anything else I can do?

<u>**DOs:**</u>
- ✓ Be honest.
- ✓ Accept responsibility.
- ✓ Use time wisely.
- ✓ Have confidence.

<u>**DON'Ts**</u>
- ✗ Have unrealistic expectations.
- ✗ Make snap decisions.
- ✗ Take unnecessary action.
- ✗ Fool yourself with band-aid fixes.

Decision-Making Scenarios

Use the decision-making steps to "advise" each student:

Scenario 1

You need a tutor for your math class. Unfortunately, the campus' learning/tutorial center is open late on the same nights you work. What will you do for the big mid-term coming up?

Scenario 2

The next semester starts in January (right after the holidays!), and you know that books are going to cost more than what your financial aid (if any) will give you. How will you fill this need?

Scenario 3

Sarah is scheduled for a nursing practicum class that means 10 hours a week next summer. Sarah has to work at least 20 hours to make it financially with her elementary aged child (home for the summer). What will Sarah do?

Scenario 4

Another student in the nursing program has just gotten a job as a volunteer in a hospital. She is required (like all volunteers and works there do) to take a drug test. Her test comes back positive for marijuana use. The volunteer coordinator says that he must report it to the college's nursing dean. What should she do?

Scenario 5

Tom's little girl is sick with flu and it's final exam day for his computer class. The test is at 1 p.m. and it's now 8 a.m. His instructor seems very strict about missing tests. The exam weighs 30% of the class grade. What should he do?

What is Your Learning Style?

Many students answer this question about what they do when they study or where they study. The learning style is much more than actions; it is how you perform best or learn a skill. Children are born with an innate learning style that begins to manifest when they are toddlers. If you watch toddlers, you will notice that some babble endlessly or are more alert to sounds around them; they may develop language skills earlier than others. Other toddlers are cued visually; they are drawn to colors, pictures or moving objects. Some toddlers are physically active all the time—they need to touch everything and may be more apt to take things apart or manipulate them. Finally, children may be more independent or more social.

As children grow or go to school, their learning styles may change based on their teachers or learning environments. Auditory learners will be told to stop moving their lips when reading. Visual learners may have difficulty sitting near windows. Kinesthetic learners will seem to fidget more or be in constant moving (not to be confused with ADD—attention deficit disorder). Unfortunately, many students may abandon their natural learning styles to perform in artificial class settings.

Now that you're an adult and attending college classes that require more self-direction, you should explore your learning styles and preferences and tap into them to become a more successful student.

On the next pages is a learning-style inventory to help you rediscover your preferred learning style. There are a number of learning inventories you can use to evaluate your learning style including the VARK and Index of Learning Styles, both of which are available for free online.

C.I.T.E. Learning Styles Instrument[1]

Circle the number that describes you for each item.

		Most like me/least like me			
1.	When I make things for my studies, I remember what I have learned better.	4	3	2	1
2.	Written assignments are easy for me to do.	4	3	2	1
3.	I learn better if someone reads a book to me than if I read silently to myself.	4	3	2	1
4.	I learn best when I study alone.	4	3	2	1
5.	Having assignment directions written on the board makes them easier to understand.	4	3	2	1
6.	It's harder for me to do a written assignment than an oral one.	4	3	2	1
7.	When I do math problems in my head, I say the numbers to myself.	4	3	2	1
8.	If I need help in the subject, I will ask a classmate for help.	4	3	2	1
9.	I understand a math problem that is written down better than one I hear.	4	3	2	1
10.	I don't mind doing written assignments.	4	3	2	1
11.	I remember things I hear better than I read.	4	3	2	1
12.	I remember more of what I learn if I learn it when I am alone.	4	3	2	1
13.	I would rather read a story than listen to it read.	4	3	2	1
14.	I feel like I talk smarter than I write.	4	3	2	1
15.	If someone tells me three numbers to add, I can usually get the right answer without writing them down.	4	3	2	1
16.	I like to work in a group because I learn from the others in my group.	4	3	2	1
		Continues on next page			

---

[1] From the Center for Innovative Teaching Experiences. Babich, A.M., Burdine, P. Allbright, L. Randal, Pl. Wichita Public School, Murdock Teacher Center

		Most like me/least like me
17.	Written math problems are easier for me to do than oral ones.	**4** **3** **2** 1
18.	Writing a spelling word several times helps me remember it better.	**4** **3** **2** 1
19.	I find it easier to remember what I heard than what I have read.	**4** **3** **2** 1
20.	It is more fun to learn with classmates at first, but it is hard to study with them.	4 3 2 1
21.	I like written directions better than spoken ones.	**4** **3** **2** 1
22.	If homework were oral, I would do it all.	**4** **3** **2** 1
23.	When I hear a phone number, I can remember it without writing it down.	**4** **3** **2** 1
24.	I get more work done when I work with someone.	**4** **3** **2** 1
25.	Seeing a number makes more sense to me than hearing a number.	**4** **3** **2** 1
26.	I like to do things like simple repairs or crafts with my hands.	**4** **3** **2** 1
27.	The things I write on paper sound better than when I say them.	**4** **3** **2** 1
28.	I study best when no one is around to talk or listen to.	**4** **3** **2** 1
29.	I would rather read things in a book than have the teacher tell me about them.	**4** **3** **2** 1
30.	Speaking is a better way than writing if you want someone to understand what you really mean.	**4** **3** **2** 1
31.	When I have a written math problem to do, I say it to myself to understand it better.	**4** **3** **2** 1
32.	I can learn more about a subject if I am with a small group of students.	**4** **3** **2** 1
33.	Seeing the price of something written down is easier for me to understand than having someone tell me the price.	**4** **3** **2** 1 Continues on next page...

		Most like me/least like me			
34.	I like to make things with my hands.	4	3	2	1
35.	I like tests that call for sentence completion or written answers.	4	3	2	1
36.	I understand more from a class discussion than from reading about a subject.	4	3	2	1
37.	I remember the spelling of a word better if I see it written down than if someone spells it out loud.	4	3	2	1
38.	Spelling and grammar rules make it hard for me to say what I want to in writing.	4	3	2	1
39.	It makes it easier when I say the numbers of a problem to myself as I work it out.	4	3	2	1
40.	I like to study with other people.	4	3	2	1
41.	When teachers say a number, I really don't understand it until I write it down.	4	3	2	1
42.	I understand what I have learned better when I am involved in making something for the subject.	4	3	2	1
43.	Sometimes I say dumb things, but writing gives me time to correct myself.	4	3	2	1
44.	I do well on tests if they are about things I hear in class.	4	3	2	1
45.	I can't think as well when I work with someone else as when I work alone.	4	3	2	1

How to score:

Fill out the totals on next page. Write the number you circled for each statement. Add and multiply the total times two. Put the final amount in the box. See the scale on the following page to interpret your results.

C.I.T.E. TOTALS

Visual Language		Social-Individual		Auditory-Numerical	
5 - _____		4 - ____		7 - ____	
13 - _____		12 - ____		15 - ____	
21 - _____		20 - ____		23 - ____	
29 - _____		28 - ____		31 - ____	
37 - _____		45 - ____		39 - ____	

Total_____ x 2 = ·_____   Total_____ x 2 = ·_____   Total____ x 2 = _____

Visual-Numerical		Social-Group		Kinesthetic-Tactile	
9 - _____		8- _____		1- _____	
17 - _____		16- _____		18 - _____	
25 - _____		24- _____		26 - _____	
33 - _____		32- _____		34 - _____	
41 - _____		40- _____		42 - _____	

Total___ x 2 =·____   Total___ x 2 =____   Total___ x 2 = _____

Auditory-Language		Expressiveness-Oral		Expressiveness-Written	
3 - _____		6 - _____		2 - _____	
11 - _____		14 - _____		10 - _____	
19 - _____		22 - _____		27 - _____	
36 - _____		30 - _____		35 - _____	
44 - _____		38 - _____		43 - _____	

Total_____ x 2 =·____   Total_____ x 2 = ·_____   Total_____ x 2 = ____ ·

*SCALE: 33-40   = Major Learning Style   21-32 = Minor Learning Style
              5-20   =Negligible Use

If you have more than one learning style, don't worry. You are a multi-modal learner who is quite flexible in various learning environments. By the way, instructors may teach in their favorite learning style, so communicate with them if you need additional learning aids. **See the next page for explanations** of how to best use your learning style!

Reflection:
  1. What results surprised you?
  2. Were you aware of your learning style?
  3. Have you ever been forced by an instructor or class setting to abandon your style? How did that affect your learning?

The Learning Environment
CITE Learning Styles[2]

Find your major and minor learning styles in the descriptions below. Read the descriptions and the strategies carefully.

Visual Language or Visual Numerical Learners	
Descriptions	**Strategies for Visual Learners**
Visual Language Learner You are someone who learns well from seeing words in books, on the chalkboard, charts or workbooks. You may even write down words that are given orally in order to learn by seeing them on paper. You remember and use information better if you have read it. **Visual Numerical Learner** You must see numbers – on the board, in a book, or on a paper – in order to work with them. You are more likely to remember and understand math facts when they are presented visually but don't need as much oral explanation.	• Take notes and use your textbooks. • Look for pictures, diagrams, charts, and graphs in your textbooks. • Avoid visually stimulating surroundings when concentrating. • Make sure you have plenty of pencils and pens, perhaps even colorful markers or highlighters! • Draw charts and graphs to make meaning of new ideas. • Use note cards. • Keep scratch paper around for math. • Use rulers or other visual aids for math. • Write down all directions

---

[2] Wisconsin Vocational Studies Center, University of Wisconsin at Madison.

Auditory Language or Auditory Numerical Learners

Descriptions	Strategies for Auditory Learners
Auditory Language Learner You are a learner who learns from hearing words spoken. You may vocalize or move your lips or throat while reading, especially when trying to understand new material. You will be more capable of understanding and remembering words or facts that could only have been learning by hearing. **Auditory Numerical Learner** You learn from hearing numbers and oral explanations. Remembering telephone and locker numbers is easy, and you may be successful with oral number games and puzzles. You may do just as well without your math book, for written materials are not important. You may be able to work problems in your head, and you may say numbers out loud when reading.	• Study where you can read aloud to yourself. • Repeat directions or instructions aloud. • When possible, sound out answers to questions or problems. • Avoid noisy places where you might be distracted. • Music might help you concentrate, but make sure it's not too wordy. • Have someone drill you aloud. • Use a computer with sounds. • Ask your teacher to tell you new things. • Say answers in your head before you commit them to paper. • Write down all directions

Auditory-Visual-Kinesthetic Learner

Description	Strategies for A-V-K Learners
You learn best by experience and being involved in your learning. You benefit from a combination of stimuli. Your learning will be aided by manipulating material along with sight and sound. You may not seem to understand or be able to concentrate on work unless you're totally involved. You seek to handle, touch, and work with what you are learning.	• Use pencils and pens that feel comfortable to the touch. • Sit in comfortable places, but avoid seats that distract you. • Use a calculator, PDA, or a computer (or a ruler to guide). • Write ideas down, then trace them with your fingers. • Draw pictures to help you learn but avoid doodling. • Hold your books or notebooks. • Read your textbooks while on a treadmill or while stretching a rubber band. Move your body as you learn. • Try doing things to help you learn. Try math problems in a store or rehearse an essay like a speech. Do science experiments or observations.

Individual Learner

Description	Strategies for Individual Learners
You get more work done alone. You think best and remember more you learn alone. You care more for your own opinions than for the ideas of others. Instructors do not have much difficulty keeping you from over-socializing in class.	• Find an isolated place to study. • Turn the phone off. • Don't be afraid to ask questions even if you like to learn it yourself. • Sit near the front of the class to make sure you get the help you need. • Quiz yourself using end of chapter tests and vocabulary lists.

Group Learner

Description	Strategies for Group Learners
You prefer to study with at least one other student and do not get much done alone. You value others' opinions and recognition of facts. Instructors will often observe you socializing in class.	• Use friends to help you study but avoid people who distract you. • Sit away from other students you like to talk to. • Study in quiet, un-peopled areas if you are being distracted. • Find a study partner who's serious. • Use the REQUEST method to study. • Make note-cards and have someone drill you.

Oral Expressive Learner

Description	Strategies for Oral Expressive Learners
You prefer to tell what you know. You talk fluently, comfortably, and clearly. You probably know more than written tests show. You are less shy than others about giving reports or talking to the instructor or classmates. Organizing and putting thoughts on paper may be too slow and tedious a task for you.	• Say or read materials aloud. • Take speech classes or offer to make a speech of your research. • Ask your instructor to give you an oral test. • Rehearse materials for a test aloud. • Record notes and play them back. • Work on a computer. • Study with a friend. • Avoid noisy places to study

Written Expressive Learner	
Description	**Strategies for Written Expressive Learners**
You can write fluent essays and good answers on tests to show what you know. You feel less comfortable when oral answers or presentations are required. Your thoughts are better organized on paper than when they are given orally.	• Write down all instructions. • Write out notes thoroughly to learn them. • Practice writing essays for tests. • Write out the words of a math problem. • Offer to do written papers for extra credit. • Ask for essay questions. • Write down questions you have for the instructor. • Have plenty of writing materials around when you work.

Learning Styles Reflection Activity

1. Do you agree with your learning style results? Why or why not?

2. What are five strategies you either currently use or will start using to take advantage of your learning style?

3. Describe your ideal study environment. Where are you? What materials do you need? Who is with you (if anyone)? Be specific.

A Crisis

Even the best organized adult student will face some unexpected or unplanned sickness, job problems, a broken-down car, a sick relative or child or a funeral. How you approach a crisis can determine how well you weather the storm and keep the crisis from fully disrupting your semester. Some tips for dealing with a crisis include:

- Communicate immediately with your instructor.
- Re-prioritize your time to include dealing with the crisis.
- Use good decision-making skills to reorganize and regroup.
- Don't give up! This is just a short set-back.

David William Furnas, M.D. suggested we look at crisis in this manner:

> "A crisis at the outset, usually augers nothing but ill. In the long run, however, my crises have more often than not marked a new course in my life, which is more fulfilling and more exciting than anything in the past.
>
> Yes, a bit of good luck is needed, but the special feature of a crisis is that you are suddenly cut off from past patterns, habits and interdependencies. Along with the distress and pain is freedom!
>
> Freedom to build again with a new foundation and modern structure, using wisdom you didn't have the last time you built." [3]

As an adult, your life will have some stops along the way. If you must "stop-out" with your education, make it a priority to return. It's never too late to continue your education!

---

[3] *Who's Who 1980-81*. Bernan Press (United Kingdom: PA); 44th edition, Jul 25, 1980.

Are You Under Stress?

Stress can be defined as "anxiety or apprehension which affects the mental and physical condition of a person." (medicine.com)   Stress is brought on by a variety of causes or circumstances experienced by an individual.   Stress can be experienced by anyone at any age including children, teens, adults and the elderly.   Stress can also be a positive force because it often causes us to learn and grow.

So why are we discussing stress in a study skills class?   School work can cause stress just like all those little problems people normally experience such as changing jobs, getting married, having children or paying bills.   Add this stress to all the others, and a student can become very uptight--so much so that he or she can't concentrate!   One common cause of stress among students is **PROCRASTINATION** which is when a student puts off completing assignments and projects then becomes stressed when due dates loom.   Use **time management** to avoid procrastination.

Here are some tips on getting rid of stress:

U nbutton your top button and breathe in and out slowly.
N ever panic! Take time to unwind before a test or assignment.
W ork on homework and assignments a little bit at a time.
I nvolve yourself in relaxing activities you like such as time with friends.
N umber your priorities! Do the most important first.
D evise a plan so that stress doesn't mount up from sudden deadlines.

In any given moment if you feel stress, stop and take a **deep** breath. Breathe in through you nose and blow the breath out very slowly through your mouth.   You should feel the enriched oxygen in your blood begin to relax your muscles and clear your mind.   Repeat up to three times.

For larger stress-filled situations, use the visualization technique on the following page to work through issues.

Using Visualization to Deal with Anxiety

TO PREPARE: Take a few deep breaths and exhale each slowly.

VISUALIZE: Close your eyes and imagine each scene, then relive each scene by ridding yourself of the anxieties. Think of dealing with the situation in the best way possible whether it means avoiding the stress, altering the stress, or accepting the stress. By doing this, you resolve the issue BEFORE it becomes stressful!

SCENE 1: If you're a facing a week with several (or one) tests, long work shifts and other stresses, imagine how you felt the last time this happened. Remember the painful muscle knots, anxious feelings, frustrations… Now imagine each of these sensations floating away. Take a deep breath and exhale.

SCENE 2: If someone is being negative about your studies or classes, remember the one time you were faced with someone else who put you down. How did you feel emotionally and physically? What would you have said? Now imagine you said what you needed to and that person backs off. Take a deep breath and exhale. Prepare to deal with your negative person.

Taking Care of Yourself

- ☐ Eat a low-fat diet with lots of foods with anti-oxidants (such as blueberries, salmon, dark chocolate, olive oil).
- ☐ Pack a healthy snack and/or lunch to carry with you to campus (High-fiber/protein bars and fruit are great!)
- ☐ Drink lots of water—carry a large bottle with you!
- ☐ Wash your hands a lot. Carry anti-bacterial cleanser.
- ☐ Alleviate, Alert, Avoid or Accept your stress.

Now take the stress test on the next page and see how you rate. Be honest!

STRESS TEST[4]

How much stress do you have?

Instructions: Take the following test to see how much stress you are facing in life right now. Check the events that have happened to you in the past year and score the points for each event you check. Add up the total.

✓ I Have	Rank	Event (in last year)	Value	My Score
	1	Death of spouse or mate	100	
	2	Divorce/separation from mate	73	
	3	Marital separation	65	
	4	Jail Term	63	
	5	Death of close family member	63	
	6	Personal injury or illness	53	
	7	Change in major or plan of study	57	
	8	Marriage	50	
	9	Loss of financial aid	48	
	10	Fired from work	47	
	11	Failing grade or failed course	47	
	12	Marital reconciliation	45	
	13	Retirement	45	
	14	Change in family member or mate's health	44	
	15	Pregnancy	40	
	16	Sexual difficulties	39	
	17	Addition to family	39	
	18	Business readjustment	39	
	19	Change in amount of income	38	
	20	Death of close friend	37	
	21	Change to different line of work	36	
	22	Change in number of family arguments	35	
	23	Mortgage or loan over $20,000	31	
continues on next page…			**Total this page**	

[4] Adapted from T.H.Holmes & R.H. Rahe. "The Social Readjustment Scale." *Campus Health Guide*. Carol Otis and Roger Goldingay. (New York: 1989).

✓ I Have	Rank	Event (in last year)	Value	My Score
	24	Foreclosure of mortgage or loan	30	
	25	Change in work responsibilities	29	
	26	Son or daughter leaving home	29	
	27	First term in college.	29	
	28	Trouble with in-laws	28	
	29	Outstanding personal achievement	26	
	30	Spouse (mate) begins or stops work	26	
	31	Starting or finishing school	25	
	32	Change in living conditions	24	
	33	Change of personal habits	23	
	34	Trouble with boss	20	
	35	Change in work hours or conditions	20	
	36	Change in residence (where you live)	20	
	37	Change in schools (you or kids)	19	
	38	Change in recreational habits	19	
	39	Change in church or church activities	18	
	40	Change in social activities	17	
	41	Mortgage or loan under $20,000	16	
	42	Change in sleeping habits	15	
	43	Change in times family get s togethers	15	
	44	Change in eating habits	14	
	45	Vacation or holiday season	13	
	46	Minor violation of the law	11	
		total this page ____ + last page =	Test total	
100-150 = 31% low stress		151-299 / 51% Some stress	299 & up / 80-90% High stress!	

Your test total gives you the percentage of the chance you will suffer physical effects directly related to your stress! If your number was higher than 31%, then you need to reduce your stress!

Reflection: Now plan ways to reduce your stress in the next few days! Write your plans in your planner.

Stressful Terminology and Practicum

Match the definition and scenario to each term:

Term	Definition	Scenario
Anxiety	**1.** This releases powerful neuro-chemicals and hormones that prepare us for action to fight or flee.	**A.** Joe loses 15 pounds over a span of half a semester.
Balance	**2.** The idea that certain amount of stress is good for an individual.	**B.** Sara takes yoga every morning before her nursing classes.
Stress	**3.** Feeling of apprehension or fear that has physical symptoms such as palpitations and sweating	**C.** Mary is taking 18 hours and working 30 every week. She has a toddler.
Capacities	**4.** Reactions include being over-aroused, short-tempered, irritable, anxious, and tense. Often, described as having "a lot of nervous energy." Always in a hurry.	**D.** Tamara has been laid off from her third job in a year and has experienced migraines.
Yerkes-Dodson Principle	**5.** A biological system that enables us to know where our bodies are in the environment and to maintain a desired position.	**E.** Sue has a midterm and a project due the same day.
Stressor	**6.** Results from demand and pressures of recent past or anticipation of future demands and pressures.	**F.** Harry exercises daily to keep up with his fire-rescue training.
Response	**7.** Occurs when life is a year-after-year grind that wears on a person's health.	**G.** Joe has to give a speech in front of a class.
Episodic Acute Stress	**8.** How the body deals with stress. This can be healthy or unhealthy	**H.** Harry is always rushing to class and is often late.
Episodic Stress	**9.** Stress as a result of being exposed to a stressor..	**I.** Sue feels nausea and has sweaty palms.
Acute stress	**10.** Any event or situation that is perceived by an individual as a threat causing us to either adapt or initiate the stress response.	**J.** Kendra has just finished her first semester and is registering for her next.
Chronic Stress	**11.** Occurs in short-term events such as a near accident	**K.** John avoids going to his mid-term in Biology.

Check the glossary for term information if needed! Answers in glossary.

:) The best way to overcome stress is to consider your overall health and wellness.

A Wellness Checklist for the College Student

The college campus brings together a variety of people of all types of backgrounds. It is collaborative atmosphere with lots of interactions and contact. That means there are many opportunities to be exposed to health risks. If your college has a nursing program, check to see if there are regular health checks for blood pressure, or blood tests for sugar or cholesterol. Many colleges offer regular, private testing for HIV as well as health fairs for wellness awareness. Read the following questions and consider how your health and wellness are being affected. Seek medical help or find ways to be healthier if you are not currently reducing your risks for a less-healthy lifestyle.

A Student's Wellness Checklist*					
	Behavior	Always	Often	Some times	Never
1.	I eat vegetables and fruits daily.				
2.	I eat fast food more than twice a week.				
3.	I drink at least 8 eight ounce glasses of water a day.				
4	I consume caffeine more than twice a day.				
5.	I wash or sanitize my hands after touching outside or public places.				
6.	I or my partner uses condoms to avoid HIV infection.				
7.	I get flu shots every new flu season.				
8.	I get a physical every year.				
9.	I know my blood pressure numbers.				
10.	I know my cholesterol numbers (low LDLs).				
11.	I exercise at least 30 minutes 3 to 5 times a week.				
12.	I practice safe sneezing and coughing.				
13.	I get at least six hours of sleep every night.				
14.	I know my stress levels (see earlier test).				
15.	I use drugs recreationally.				
16.	I smoke cigarettes.				

Students should practice the same healthy habits as any adult, but often they are too busy with their academics and forget to think about their physical or emotional well-being. Obviously, getting plenty of sleep, eating well, staying hydrated and avoiding stress are good first steps. Since the college campus can mean contact with sick classmates, it is best to sanitize hands and get regular shots!

*This is not a guaranteed health check, just a few questions to get you to think about this vital part of your student life. Check online for additional surveys or see your private physician or clinician for wellness checks.

Practicum and Scenarios

Read the following scenarios and provide suggestions of how that student could avoid the negative or stressful behavior.

1. Sue is a visual and auditory learner. She was told to go to the library to study for her classes, but she finds herself not remembering what she's read or being unable to complete work. She sits at the tables near the front desk and doors. All her friends know this is where she studies, and they often seek her company there. What could Sue do?

2. Harry's girlfriend is not in college, but she says she supports his decision to be a full-time student after he reduced his work schedule from 40 to 20 hours a week. She spends a lot of time at his two-bedroom apartment (which he shares with three other students). He has a major project due this week and two papers due next; his girlfriend reminds him that it will be her birthday in two days, and he promised to take her out. What can Harry do?

3. Lulu's instructor lectures for an hour and half twice a week. She must read three chapters for each week's class. Lulu has a difficult time remembering the details of her class in order to prepare for tests. What can Lulu do? (think of the topics covered in this chapter).

4. Bob wants to be a straight-A student. He is taking 18 hours (or 6 classes) this semester. He just found out his mother is ill, so he will need to help her out at least 21 hours a week. What should Bob do?

5. Tim does his classwork every day before he takes an hour-long bus ride to campus. He realizes today that he left his two papers on his desktop computer before he came to campus today. This means another 5 points off for each assignment, and it's the second time this semester he's forgotten the work he completed. What should Tim do in the future?

What the Students Say...

…the most important attribute a student can have is a positive attitude… Participation in class…a student does not necessarily have to voice in on every topic…but should demonstrate …paying attention and offer comments relevant to the conversation. MS (2008)

My favorite place is lying on my bed, just chilling. I will turn off both of my phones to make sure I don't get side-tracked. I will turn on some soft-playing music and just let my hand write away… BJ (2008)

…my strengths as a student are organization, turning in work on time, being courteous and respectful. JW (2008)

…making a good grade in class feels awesome. I know then that all my studying was worth the effort. It relieves the pressure of wondering about the grade. FJ (2008)

Chapter 4
Career
Exploration

Career Choices
Personality Types
Work Values
Campbell Interest Survey

Thinking About My Career

Directions: Check the scale that describes your knowledge of your skills or decisions about your career.

Very sure	Almost Sure	A little sure	Not sure	
				I have chosen a program of study.
				I know where I want to be in my career in 5 years.
				I know where I want to be in my career in 10 years.
				My interests fit my career.
				My skills fit my career.
				My career matches my values.
				My career will satisfy my highest desires.
				This college will train me for my career.
				I will need to do more education than this college offers
				I have the time needed to pursue my education.
				The classes I am taking now will help me with my career.
				I am creative.
				I like to make decisions for others.
				I know where the career services office is.
				I will want to do my chosen career until I retire.
				I'm excited about being in college.
				I love math or science.
				I like nature and being outdoors.
				Adventure is what I seek.
				I know someone doing my chosen career.
				I think then act.
				I feel the situation out before I act.
				I like working alone.
				I want others to approve of my work and choices.
				My parents/family want me to pursue this career.
				I want to work in an office.

Do the following inventories and surveys, then compare them in the chart at the end of this chapter. Don't get upset if you find your current choice for a career is not what you find at the end of this chapter. Continue to explore and research. You will find the correct path!

What Career? What Degree? Which College?

Have you decided on your career choice? You may already be employed in the area in which you seek a degree, diploma or certificate. You may be just enhancing skills you've acquired "on the job," or you may be seeking licensure or credentials to demonstrate expertise you have. No matter your goal, it is a good idea to explore your career choice.

Some people do not decide what career they want until well into their late twenties or thirties while others may face a career change in their forties and fifties. A few stay-at-home parents may wait until their children are older before they pursue college degrees or careers while some hard-working blue collar workers need to change their careers due to health or physical limitations. Basically, everyone needs to look as his/her career life.

There are a number of factors and reasons someone pursues a career. It can include many of the following:

- Family or life history
- Personal interests
- Personal talents or skills
- Personality
- Values
- Education/training experiences
- Financial need
- Physical or health restrictions or skills
- Learning style
- Market need for workers
- Location desire

You have explored your educational attitude and learning style. Your personal history is something for your own consideration. A good place to start is your college's career counseling center. Visit a job fair that targets potential employees for a particular career. Talk to someone at the Employment Security Commission about job openings and required training. Interview someone in your career or shadow a person doing the work you're interested in. The community colleges offer a great deal of training in various areas. On the following page is a list of potential careers and the degrees, diplomas and certificates required. Of course, there always new careers and training be added as our world and her population needs change.

After examining the career list, let's look at some work values and personality traits to see how they match your career choice(s).

Community College Programs and Training

Scan the following areas offered by many colleges. In some states, such as North Carolina, programs may not be duplicated college located in the same area. Other programs, such as nursing, are in high demand; therefore, multiple colleges, despite location, will offer training in similar areas. Review the type of types of credentials before you look at the programs. These range from as many as 75 credit hours to as few as 15 credit hours. There also some shorter programs that offer refresher courses; your local small business center will have many of these one- or two-day seminars or workshops. Finally, your current employer may access the local college to provide additional training to boost work skills including areas such as firefighting, police, computers, medical fields and education or to provide recertification in these fields.

Credential	Hours to Complete	Length of Program
Certificate	18	1-2 semesters
Diploma	36	2-3 semesters
Associate's Of Applied Science Of Arts Of Science Degree in Nursing	64-68 For a specific career For transfer into a bachelor's For transfer into a bachelor's ADN for RNs	4-6 semesters
Bachelor's Of Arts Of Science	124-160 For areas such as Education, sociology, history, etc. For areas in science, math or accounting	8-10 semesters
Master's	30+	2-8 semesters

Don't forget that the Bachelor's degree is earned at a four-year school, of which you may transfer half from your university transfer program earned with an associate's degree. Some colleges have a time-limit for a course's credits being accepted (in other words the credits may expire or need repeating). Most colleges require that their students make steady progress in their programs. Finally, look at the bi-lateral agreements made between two-year and four-year institutions, where additional hours earned outside a specific study-track may actually transfer toward a bachelor's major or a minor degree area.

Your college courses have numbers. The order may indicate pre-requisite courses while others (those below 100) do not carry transfer credit or count towards your career major. Your overall GPA will include all coursework (even though failed), but your major area GPA will not have courses with a number under 100 or failed courses since you will not be granted the degree with failed coursework. It always best to check with YOUR COLLEGE for specific information about course numbers and GPA calculations.

Now let's look at the many program areas available at community colleges (please be aware this is not a comprehensive list). In North Carolina alone, there are over a 1,000 curriculum areas broken to over 250 curriculum areas (www.ncccommunitycolleges.edu). Additional programs may be added for regional needs or student demands. (www.nccommunitycolleges.edu) The curriculum programs are organized under the following areas in North Carolina:

Arts and Sciences
Associate in General Education
Agricultural and Natural Resources Technologies
Biological and Chemical Technologies
Business Technologies
Commercial and Artistic Production Technologies
Construction Technologies
Engineering Technologies
Health Science
Industrial Technologies
Public Service Technologies
Transportation Systems Technologies
Source: www.nccommunitycolleges.edu

The following curriculum areas are categorized by credential type; please note that many of the programs under the associate category also have diploma or certificate credential in specialized areas. Check the program's plan of study (review chapter one if needed) to see what core and major courses are required. In many cases, the core courses are the same across program curriculum. Contact your local community college to see if a particular area is offered.

Certificate Credential   (16-19 hrs)

Community or Medical Spanish Facilitator	Computer Information Technology – Linux + and CLP
Spanish Language	Computer Programming – Database Programming, Software Specialist
Accounting Bookkeeper/entrepreneur	Computer Programming – Visual C#, Visual Basic or JAVA
Law Enforcement	Computer Information Technology – Microsoft
Early Childhood	Information Systems Security – Security Network
Architectural Tech--CAD	Networking Technology – CCNA or Network +
Automotive Tech—electrical, machining, drive train, etc.	Office Systems Administration – Word Processing
Electronics Engineering Technology – Computer Repair	Dental Laboratory Technology – Dental Ceramics Techniques, Bridgework, etc.
Electrical/ Electronics Technology – Construction Electrician	Medical Assisting – Introductory Medical Assisting or Office Centered
Electrical/ Electronics Technology – Control or Maintenance Electrician	Pharmacy Technology – Retail Pharmacy Technician
Industrial Systems Technology – Introductory HVAC	Phlebotomy
Industrial Systems Technology – Introductory Welding	Truck Driver Training
Machining Technology – Automotive, Basic, or CNC Machining,	Web Technologies – Web Designer
Clinical Trials Research Associate – Level 1. Level 2, Data Management	

Diploma Credential (32-48 hrs)

Automotive Technology	Plumbing
Health Information Technology – Comprehensive Coding	Carpentry
Machining Technology	Boat Building
Medical Assisting	Heavy Equipment Operator
Pharmacy Technology	Marine Propulsion Systems
Practical Nursing	Motorcycle Mechanics
Surgical Technology	Small Engine and Equipment Repair
Masonry	Dental Assisting

Associate Credential (64-70 hrs)

Biotechnology	Respiratory Therapy
General Education	Fine Arts (Drama, Music)
Business Administration Technology	Gaming Management
Early Childhood	Travel and Tourism Technology
Architectural Technology	Paralegal Technology
Automotive Systems Technology	Hotel and Restaurant Management
Electronic Engineering	Real Estate
Electrical/ Electronics Technology	Commercial Refrigeration Technology
Industrial Systems Technology	Aviation Systems Technology
Computer Programming	Race Car Technologies
Computer Information Technology	Cardiovascular Sonography
Health Information Technology	Dental Hygiene
Information Systems Security	Human Services Technology
Networking Technology	Occupational Therapy Assistant
Office Systems Administration	Therapeutic Massage
Medical Office Administration	Occupational Therapy Assistant
Web Technologies	Opticianry
Associate Degree Nursing	Radiography
Clinical Trials Research Associate	Respiratory Therapy
Dental Laboratory Technology (75 hrs)	Speech-Language Pathology Assistant

Use the *Occupational Outlook Handbook* online or go to other career sites (check your library for databases!) to investigate career opportunities and salaries. Take the following inventories to see if your interests and personality trait match your career choice.

What Interests You?

In Vince Lombardi's *Babysteps to Success*, a question is asked, "What do you enjoy doing so much that you would do it for <u>free</u>?" This could be an indicator of your career future. If your hobbies or leisure activities are those you pursue with great motivation and time investment, then perhaps you can integrate them into your future career. That doesn't necessarily mean that if you like twittering your friends about your feelings you should pursue a career in twittering, but this could indicate a skill in interpersonal relationships and jobs that require such skills as in nursing or education or even business administration.

Many career counseling centers on campuses offer career interest inventories. Career counselors can help students choose careers that best suit their personality, interests, values and skills. The next few pages will help you self-assess these components of yourself.

With the high cost of education, it is not wise to just experiment in many different areas of study until something clicks or feels right, make choices based on real career possibilities. It is also common that adults will get training or degrees in areas in which they can, for a time, earn enough money for their life and family needs then go back to school for additional training and degrees to further pursue their "perfect" careers.

Myers-Briggs Personality

The Myer-Briggs Personality Types Inventory is a good source of information to review how you learn, think and interact with people in various situations. Businesses often use the inventory to help employees see how they can work together better. The four types, based on Carl Jung's original research, are intuitive or sensing, extroversion or introversion, thinking or feeling, and judging or perceiving. Below are some characteristics of each of these types.

characteristics	Intuitive (N) ○ Future possibilities ○ Patterns & connections ○ Theories ○ Guessing from memory ○ Imagination & creation	Sensing (S) ○ Here & now ○ Facts from past ○ Concrete facts ○ Common sense ○ Practical
	Extroversion (E) ○ Act then think ○ Interact with world ○ Motivated by world ○ Variety of relationships	Introversion (I) ○ Think then act ○ Need time alone ○ Inner motivation ○ One to one relationships
	Thinking (T) ○ Search for facts ○ Task oriented ○ Accepts conflict ○ Objective	Feeling (F) ○ Use personal feelings ○ Sensitive to others ○ Seeks other's approval ○ Subjective
	Judging (J) ○ Plans ahead ○ Aims for completion ○ Meets deadlines early ○ Likes routine	Perceiving (P) ○ Plan on-the-go ○ Multi tasking ○ Work close to deadline ○ Variety and freedom

Study Skill Practice: Go back and highlight two characteristics you have in this chart. Then annotate in the margin how this affects your behavior in the classroom (think of discussions, participation, or group activities).

(more on next page…)

Your type will be a four-point result such as **INTJ.** You can take this inventory online at various websites such as *www.humanmetrics.com/cgi-win/JTypes1.htm*. Some sites will give you a career link to your results.

While there is no perfect correlation between your personality type and your chosen career, there may be some link to how happy you may be or how well you persist in your career choice. This is the time to consider how to best fit your college major and your personality tendencies.

You can also use your results to evaluate your study habits, effort, motivation and time management. Once you've identified your traits, you can work to modify how you approach your college work. Your personality traits do not dictate your choices or habits, but they strongly influence your daily life; therefore, they will influence your student life and goal management.

Reflection:

1. Which of your personality traits or characteristics have negative effects on your student life?

2. How can you change or meet head-on the challenges these create?

Self-Assessment: Holland Codes

Holland Codes are a widely known and well-respected personality and interest assessment. Dr. John Holland, a psychologist, identified the six personality types below that can be combined into 720 different personality patterns. These types refer to both individual personalities and workplace environments.

Career counselors recommend identifying your personal Holland Codes and then looking for similar work environments. People who work in environments that match their personality types are more likely to feel satisfied in their work lives. Both the *Occupational Outlook Handbook* (www.bls.gov/oco) and College Foundation of North Carolina (www.cfnc.org) websites refer to Holland Codes.

The Holland Codes are typically presented using the hexagon below to show the relationships of the codes to one another. The codes closest together are more alike; the codes opposite from each other are least alike. Most people are a combination of types, and the combinations usually correspond with each other on the hexagon.

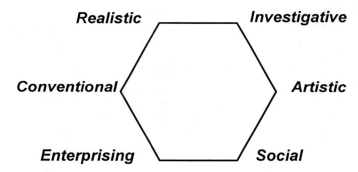

Once you determine your Holland Code (see next page), use the chart below to identify your compatible work environments. You'll see that the compatibility is determined by the location on the hexagon.

Personality Type	Most Compatible	Compatible
Realistic	Realistic	Investigative & Conventional
Investigative	Investigative	Realistic & Artistic
Artistic	Artistic	Investigative & Social
Social	Social	Artistic & Enterprising
Enterprising	Enterprising	Social & Conventional
Conventional	Conventional	Enterprising & Realistic

Source:
www.careerkey.org/asp/your_personality/hollands_theory_of_career_choice.asp

What is your Holland Code?

Read the descriptions below and decide which personality type defines you the best. Next, choose which would be second and third best descriptions of your personality. Now write the three letters below. This is your Holland Code: ____   ____   ____

R - Realistic People
(Doers)

They like to work with machines, and they often like to work with their hands to build things. Their skills include having mechanical know-how, stamina to work outdoors, and the ability to operate machinery. They are often practical, love nature, and are good problem solvers. They like working with things and tools.

I - Investigative People
(Thinkers)

They like to explore ideas and analyze data. They have skills in math and science. Inquisitive, precise, and sometimes abstract thinking are characteristics of their personality. They usually like working with data and ideas.

C - Conventional People
(Organizers)

They like an organized and detail-oriented work place. They are often skilled in finance, mathematics, and keyboarding, and see themselves as conforming, organized, and practical. They like working with data.

A - Artistic People
(Creators)

They like to create, sing, dance, or write and prefer an unstructured work environment. They have skills in music, art, and/or communication. They value aesthetic qualities and are more likely to relate by indirect means through their medium. They like working with ideas.

E - Enterprising People
(Persuaders)

They like to persuade and influence others in areas of business or politics. They perceive themselves as popular, self-confident, and social. They are skills in public speaking and leadership. Enterprising types like working with people and data.

S - Social People
(Helpers)

They enjoy helping others and the community. They have skills in teaching, counseling, and getting along with others, and are sensitive to others' needs. They are cheerful, scholarly, and verbally oriented. They like working with people.

Careers According to the Holland Codes

Every profession requires more than just one talent. The chart below only shows the main characteristics of each career or workplace environment. Remember that according to the theory behind the Holland Codes, you should look for a workplace environment that is compatible with your personal Holland Code.

R - Realistic Careers (Doers)

engineer, broadcast technician, landscape worker, barber, fire fighter, cook, auto mechanic, carpenter, surgical technologist, machinist, heavy truck driver, pest control worker, air traffic controller, roofer

I - Investigative Careers (Thinkers)

computer programmer, conservation scientist, financial analyst, microbiologist, physician, physician's assistant, pharmacist, chemist, biomedical engineer, food scientist, veterinarian, natural sciences manager, geologist, anthropologist, lab technician

C - Conventional Careers (Organizers)

bookkeeper/accountant, tax preparer, court reporter, cashiers, paralegal, bank teller, insurance underwriter, medical records technician, secretary/office worker, building inspector, computer operator

A - Artistic Careers (Creators)

commercial artist, singer, actor/actress, editor, author, music teacher, journalist, graphic designer, advertising manager, floral designer, animator, museum curator, photographer

E - Enterprising Careers (Persuaders)

sales person, financial manager, construction manager, sports promoter, convention manager, lawyer, politician, real estate agent, marketing manager, business executive

S - Social Careers (Helpers)

nurse, physical therapist, occupational therapy assistant, teacher or teacher assistant, aerobics instructor, social worker, clergy, coach, dental hygienist, counselor, probation officer, paramedic, personnel director, home health aide

Reflection:
1. What is your best Holland Code?
2. How is your chosen career reflective of that code?
3. Who will you work best with?

Self-Assessment: Work Values

The following self-assessment will give you some information about what types of satisfaction you expect from your work. Identifying your work values (like knowing your Holland Code) will help you make deliberate decisions about your future career. Not surprisingly, if you choose a career that matches your work values, then you are more likely to feel satisfied by your work.

Directions: Read the following list of satisfying results that individuals report getting from their careers. Rate the importance of each category using the following scale:

1	Unimportant or undesirable
2	Somewhat important
3	Very important to you in your career/job

Rate | **Career Value**

_____ Advancement: Have opportunities to work hard and move ahead in my organization

_____ Affiliation: Be recognized as being associated with a particular organization

_____ Artistic: Be involved in creative works of art, music, literature, drama, decorating, or other art forms

_____ Authority: Have control over others' work activities and be able to partially affect their destinies

_____ Be Needed: Feel that what I do is necessary for the survival or welfare of others

_____ Beauty: Have a job which involves the aesthetic appreciation of the study of things, ideas, or people

_____ Community: Work at a job in which I can get involved in community affairs

Rate | **Career Value**

_____ Location: Live in a place which is conducive to my lifestyle and in which I can do many of the activities I enjoy

_____ Moral/spiritual: Have a sense that my work is important to and in accord with a set of standards in which I believe

_____ Orderliness of Environment: Work in a consistently ordered environment where everything has its place and things are not changed often

_____ Personal Growth and Development: Engage in work which offers me opportunity to grow as a person

_____ Physical Work Environment: Work in a place which is pleasing to me aesthetically or beautiful to me

_____ Physical: Do work which makes physical demands and I which I can use my coordination and physical abilities
>**continued on next pg.**

_____ Predictability: Have a stale and relatively unchanging work routine and job duties

128

Rate	Career Value	Rate	Career Value

Competition: Pit my abilities against those of others in situations which test my competencies and in which there are win or lose outcomes

Contact With People: Have day to day contact with the public

Creative Expression: Have opportunities to express my ideas, reactions, and observations about my work and how I might improve it verbally or in writing

Creativity: Create new programs and systems; develop original structures and procedures not dependent on someone else's format

Decision-Making: Have the power to decide policies, agendas, courses of action, etc.

Exercise Competence: Have opportunities to involve myself in those areas in which I feel I have talents above the average person

Expertise: Be respected and sought after for my knowledge and skills in a given area

Fun: Work in a situation in which I am free to be spontaneous, playful, humorous, and exuberant

Help Society: Make a contribution for the betterment of the world in which I live

Helping Others: Provide a service to and assist others as individuals or as groups

Pressure: Have a job which involves working against time deadlines and/or where others critique the quality of my work

Problem Solving: Have a position that provides challenging problems to solve and avoids routine

Productive: Produce tangibles, things I can see and touch

Recognition: Be visibly and publicly appreciated and given credit for the equality of my work

Relationships: Develop close friendships with my co-workers and other people I meet in the course of my work activities

Responsibility: Be responsible for the planning and implementation of many tasks and projects as well as for the people involved

Risk Taking: have work which requires me to take risks or challenges frequently

Security: Be able to depend on keeping my job and making enough money

Status: Have a position which carries respect with my friends, family, and community

Supervision: Be directly responsible for work which is done and produced by others under my supervision

>continued on next pg.

Rate	**Career Value**	Rate	**Career Value**

High Income Possibilities: Work, which can lead to substantial earnings or profit, enabling me to purchase essential items and the luxuries of life I desire

——

Independence: Be able to direct and control the course of my work, determining its nature without a great deal of direction from others

——

Influence: Be able to change and influence others' attitudes or opinions

——

Integration: Be able to integrate my working life with my personal life, involving my family or close friends

——

Intellectual Status: Be recognized as a person with high intellectual ability; one who is an authority in a given area of knowledge

——

Job Tranquility: Avoid pressure and the "rat race"

——

Learning: Be able to continually learn new skills and acquire new knowledge and understanding

——

Time freedom: Be free to plan and manage my own time schedule in work; be able to set my own hours

——

Undemanding: Have work duties which demand very little energy or involvement

——

Uniqueness: Feel that the work I do is unique, novel, and different from others in some way

——

Variety: Do a number of different tasks; have the setting and content of my work responsibilities change frequently

——

Work Alone: Work by myself on projects and tasks

——

Work on Frontiers of Knowledge: Be involved in hard science of human research; work in a company that is considered one of the best in the business and strive for advances

——

Work With Others: Be a member of a working team; work with others in a group toward common goals

——

This self-assessment adapted from an activity used by SOICC – North Carolina's Career Resource Network. For more information about SOICC, see www.soicc.state.nc.us.

Use the worksheet on the next page to reflect on this self-assessment.

Understanding Your Work Values

List your most important work values in any order below:

1. _____   6. _____

2. _____   7. _____

3. _____   8. _____

4. _____   9. _____

5. _____   10. _____

Choose the five values that you would **not be willing** to compromise beginning with your most valued:

1. _____

2. _____

3. _____

4. _____

5. _____

Questions for Reflection:

1. How well does your intended career match your work values? Identify your work values that will be achieved in your chosen career.

2. How does your life now reflect these values? Consider how you spend your time – do you spend time on activities that reflect your values?

3. If some of your activities or behaviors do not reflect your values, how can you change them to better reflect your values?

4. How can you apply these work values to being a college student? For example, if you value variety, how can you incorporate variety into your experiences as a college student to feel more satisfied in this area of your life?

The Campbell Interest and Skill Survey

Just like the Myers-Briggs personality types and the Holland Codes, the CISS can help you consider career areas. Below are some basic areas to consider:

Activity I would like to do:	Career Area related to that skill/activity:	Rate 1-7: with 1 being most interested in
Influencing	Law or politics Sales or advertising Leadership careers	
Organizing	Supervision Financial service Office work	
Helping	Adult development Social work Education Counseling Religious work Medical practice	
Creating	Art or design Performance arts Writing Fashion Culinary arts	
Analyzing	Computer Mathematics Sciences	
Producing	Mechanical craft Farming or forestry Animal care Gardening	
Adventuring	Athletics or physical fitness Military Law Enforcement	

Of course, you may want to combine interests such as being a medic in the military or animal behaviorist. This is just another survey to locate your career path. If your community college choice does not have this career major, then you will need to research universities or other training.

Putting It All Together

Look at your surveys and research and fill in the following. Do they match? How can you combine interests, values, needs and careers to your college work?

Program or major	Career Choice(s)	CISS (p.___)	Holland Code (pg.___)	Myers-Briggs (pg.___)	Personal Values & Needs	Work Values (pg.___)

Reflection:

What modifications will you need to make your career choice to fulfill/use your interests, skills and values?

Have you chosen the correct program to meet this career goal?

What the Students Say...

"Since I learned about SMART goals in this class, I've written SMART goals for my life as a student, my life as a mother, and my life as a bank teller!" (2008)

"I didn't realize that every small decision I make at Durham Tech will help me prepare for my new career. I've already scheduled an appointment with my advisor to make sure that I am on track to graduate on time." (2008)

"I now have the tools I need to make a seamless transfer to University of North Carolina in two years." (2009)

"I didn't know that there are so many programs at a community college." (2009)

Chapter 5
Reading Skills and Study Techniques

Reading Concepts
The Reading Task
The Active Learning Cycle
Note-taking
Annotation
SQ3R
Request
Critical Thinking

What are Your Reading Habits?

Directions: Write **A** in the row next to the examples of active reading habits and **P** in the row next to the examples of passive reading habits. When you are finished, put a check mark in the rows that describe something that you do.

Reading Habit	A or P	√
Have a positive attitude towards reading		
Read only words		
Avoid doing textbook assignment until before test		
Use scanning at appropriate times		
Use skimming instead of study-reading		
Ask questions to guide my reading and thinking		
Am unaware that reading is a process I can change		
Read only when I have time		
Read because I have to		
Expect the author to interest and motivate me		
Control my concentration		
Use study systems and memory strategies		
Underline and annotate reading materials		
Make graphic organizers to use as study guides		
See no connection between reading and life/work		
Review by re-reading entire chapters		
Seek help as needed		

Reading in the College Program

No matter what your learning style is, as a student you will do tremendous amounts of reading. This will include textbooks, articles, journals, reference materials and Internet research. A great deal of educational material comes in the form of the textbook. Most colleges require students to purchase their books. Bookstores can provide both used and new, or texts can be ordered online. Textbooks tend to be expensive since they are specialty books with smaller customer-bases. Textbooks are written by experts in the field of study which means these can be detailed and very long. Many of the textbooks writers are not instructors, so the books may not be as engaging or learning-centered as your instructor or class environment. You will need to self-motivate to push yourself through some of your major course reading!

Reading can include skimming and scanning as well as detailed study reading. **Skimming** is what you do to complete a quick overview of material. This would be a minimal start to prepare for the topic in your instructor's next class or lecture. It would provide you with some working vocabulary for note-taking and help you decide when to listen-closely to your instructor's lecture and demonstration. **Scanning** is what you do to look up information quickly to answer a question or prepare for research; you often **scan** the Internet to locate sites of use.

Study-reading is the main process by which the student gains knowledge for application. This is when the reader seeks out the main idea and its supporting details. Definitions, steps in a process and background are found in this type of reading. The reader should correlate the text with in-class information or notes and synthesize into his/her thinking and knowledge base. This is also where the essay questions and analyzing problems are derived for exams, labs, or internship practice. This activity is the most time-consuming in the homework or out-of-class assignments, but it is where the instructor expects that students will "fill-in" the extra details not covered in the class setting. Additionally, this type of reading is truly the substance of an online course where there is no actual in-class participation with an instructor; in this type of class, the study-reading must be done before online discussions or other assignments are completed. If you have large amounts of study-reading to accomplish, break the work up into smaller chunks, so you will remember more. Use the 15-5 method, where you read and study for 15 minutes and break for 5 minutes; this will allow your mind to absorb material more fully and help you refresh for each amount you cover. Using a highlighter and annotation will also help you prepare the text for review later. Sticky note outlining will provide you with "moveable" notes to add to lecture notes or research.

Vocabulary development is all part of the serious study-reading and career skill-building you will do through your semesters in college. Some students may believe that vocabulary work is for high-schoolers, but in reality, adult professionals add new words to their reading and working skills constantly. Your reading vocabulary, by far, should be your largest working vocabulary (next to your listening vocabulary). Try to add a few words every week to your repertoire. Use them in sentences aloud or write them over and over to set them deeply into your long-term memory. While it may seem that the vocabulary is restricted to a course you're taking currently; however, later in your career, you will be called to use those words in your professional life!

Be encouraged and be persistent in your reading! The more you read the more skilled you'll become. Research has shown that it takes 100 hours to strengthen your skills to the next level. While you may have only read at a high school level (somewhere between a ninth to twelfth grade level) when you graduated from secondary school, you will develop a stronger college-level skills as you read text after text each semester.

Though college reading may seem long and difficult, students cannot just avoid or skip this activity. Stay focused as you complete reading assignments, and do not get behind. There is nothing to be gained (and all to lose) if you have chapters of reading to do just before an exam. Instructors expect students to read the textbook as well as take notes from lecture for incorporating information in a course. Following are several reading techniques to help you excel in your college reading.

Reading Concepts and Terminology

As you approach the reading task and work on study techniques, there are some basic concepts you will begin to hear about often. Following are some brief explanations and definitions of these concepts or terms.

Main idea. The main idea of a passage or paragraph is the most important point an author is trying to make. As the paragraph or passage progresses, the author will use details to support the main idea.

The main idea of a paragraph is usually found in the **topic sentence** (it may be repeated in the conclusion). The main idea of a passage is usually found in the first paragraph and is sometimes called the **thesis statement**.

A **concept** is an idea or thought the author is trying to explain.

Details are examples, definitions, facts or opinions used to support the main idea.

Theory is something taken to be true without proof. *Synonym*: assumption, premise, thesis, presumption, supposition, presupposition, surmise, postulate, postulation.

Hypothesis A belief used as the basis for action. *Synonym*: supposition

Paraphrasing is the restatement of concepts or ideas in a shorter form than the original writing.

Restatement is saying or writing concepts or ideas in your own words.

Summarizing is taking the main points or highlights of a piece and restating these in shortened forms.

Exercise: *Restate or paraphrase each statement:*

1.   The early bird gets the worm.

2.   A bird in the hand is worth two in the bush.

3.   It takes two to tango.

4.   Don't let the cat out of the bag.

5.   Sally was so sick that she irritated everyone in the house.

6.   Too many cooks in the kitchen can spoil the broth.

7.   If you can't stand the heat, get out of the kitchen.

8.   President Clinton worked very hard to convince Congress that his crime bill would help solve the severe problem facing the inner city and the violence perpetuated by career criminals on the loose.

9.   He's a knight in shining armor.

10.   John went and bought a new truck after he interviewed for a new job.

Summarize the following excerpt:

Declaration of Independence
(Adopted in Congress 4 July 1776)
The Unanimous Declaration of the Thirteen United States of America

When, in the course of human events, it becomes necessary for one people to dissolve the political bonds which have connected them with another, and to assume among the powers of the earth, the separate and equal station to which the laws of nature and of nature's God entitle them, a decent respect to the opinions of mankind requires that they should declare the causes which impel them to the separation. We hold these truths to be self-evident, that all men are created equal, that they are endowed by their Creator with certain unalienable rights, that among these are life, liberty and the pursuit of happiness. That to secure these rights, governments are instituted among men, deriving their just powers form the consent of the governed.

Fact Versus Opinion

An author of any piece, whether it is fiction or nonfiction, expresses his/her opinion or attitude toward the subject. This is often called bias, but every human being has some bias because each of us is unique in our thoughts and experiences. The writer of a text can use a mix of fact and opinion in the passage or book. It is important to know the difference in order to separate fact from opinion.

An **opinion** is the statement of a writer's or author's idea. It may include a quality or emotional state in its wording.

KEY WORDS: best, worst, always, never
adjective qualifiers such as most/more beautiful
problems, concerns, difficulties
I think…I believe…

A **fact** can be quantified or measured in some way. It may be the simple description of a truth or reality.

Examples: Twenty-two hundred people voted for a gun control law.
A dog **is** a canine with **four** legs.

Activity:

A.   Determine whether each statement is an opinion or fact. Underline the key word which helps you identify what kind of statement it is.

_____1.   Reading is a difficult activity.
_____2.   A fast reader can read five hundred words a minute.
_____3.   Note-taking is the most important skill one can learn for college.
_____4.   Fifty percent of high school students cannot take notes.
_____5.   If you take the best notes you will make the best grades.
_____6.   This activity is the hardest you have done so far.

B.   Write **three opinion** AND **three factual** statements about your favorite holiday. Pair up with a classmate and see if he or she can tell the difference between your statements about your favorite holiday? How could he or she tell?

Author's Tone

Everything you read has a tone and attitude that the author is trying to express about the subject. In literature, you can see tone (author's view or emotional response) in the setting, characters, themes, mood, and plot.

Read the following:

It was a dark night, a storm raging outside the house. I crept along the corridor with my gun drawn, pressed close to my shoulder and cocked for immediate action. I had followed the skulking man inside after he had left the park. He was wanted for attacking several women, and that alone made me nervous. Despite my having a gun and a black belt, something shivered me inside to think I was tracking a rapist. He could violate me just as my stepfather had years ago.

Can you pick out the mood? What is author's attitude?

Non-fictional writing also expresses an author's attitude. If he or she is upbeat, the language will be upbeat. If he or she is critical or negative, then the language will be darker, more critical.

Read the following:

NASA scientists have released vital information on the latest satellite findings on Saturn's moon, Io. Early finding indicate there is microbic life on the surface of the moon. Although extremely cold, the surface is covered in a layer of carbon dioxide ocean that harbors frozen life. This report may confirm scientists' theories that the huge planet is a dead sun with moon-sized planets circling it.

Go back and highlight words or phrases that show the attitude/tone of the writer.

Tone is important because it affects the reader who will often adopt the same tone as he or she reads the information. As you study-read material, stop for a moment and see if you can determine the tone. When you do, you will pick out the bias the author relates. Remember, we are all biased, so read with a critical eye and mind!

The Reading Task
Five Important Steps

There are certain basic steps you should take while you read. As you read the steps, consider whether you are doing these now or are there steps you should add to your reading skills.

STEP 1: WHAT IS THE ASSIGNMENT?
Write it down.
Ask for clarifying information such as:
- ✓ When is it due?
- ✓ What are the requirements?
- ✓ How will it be evaluated?
- ✓ What are the specific pages, chapters, etc.?

STEP 2: HOW WILL MY INSTRUCTOR FOLLOW UP?
- ✓ A quiz (pop or other)?
- ✓ A discussion (questions given ahead of time)?
- ✓ A worksheet or assigned questions?
- ✓ A writing assignment?
- ✓ A unit exam?

STEP 3: WHAT TYPES OF STUDY AIDS HAVE BEEN PROVIDED?
- ✓ Ask for study sheets or guides.
- ✓ Study notes from class.
- ✓ Websites provided by the instructor or textbook.
- ✓ Look at chapter questions in the book.
- ✓ Look at vocabulary blocks or definitions.
- ✓ Use aids both before, during and after.

Continued on next page

STEP 4: **WHAT KIND OF QUESTIONS WILL I NEED TO ANSWER?**
Questions from:
- ✓ class notes
- ✓ at the end of the chapter in book
- ✓ worksheets
- ✓ study guides

STEP 5: **HOW SHOULD I READ IT?**
- ✓ Skim for general ideas or impressions.
- ✓ Scan for specific bits of information.
- ✓ Study reading with pauses for reflective thinking or note-taking.

Reflection:

1. Write down 3 or four things you already do when you're given a reading assignment:

2. Write down two things you would like to add to your skills:

3. What things do you feel you do well when you read?

The Active Learning Cycle

Reading to learn requires a different set of processes than leisure or recreational reading. Study these **six** phases and compare them to how you might approach textbook or subject reading or listening closely to a class discussion or lecture.

Phase one:

The learner **pre-reads**, **hypothesizes**, and **sets questions** to be answered about the reading or listening activity so that purposes can be established for the learning task.

I am reading about _____ therefore I will be
learning _____.

Phase two:

The learner reads or listens for key concepts that answer those already-established purposes.

I am reading or listening for_____.

Phase three:

The learner notes in some form, mentally or with some physical aid such as notes, those key concepts and special interrelationships in his/her own words.

I will note key concepts by _____.

(continued on next page)

Phase four:

The learner organizes and synthesizes the material read or listened to into an appropriate retrieval strategy for the future.

I will organize the learned material by _____.

Phase five:

The learner rehearses the material for eventual evaluation or use of the new material by either oral or written recitation, or by relating what is new to what is already known.

I will rehearse the information for _____.

Phase six:

The learner utilizes the new information in the near or distant future.

I will use the information _____.

HINT
Try using each of the fill-in-the-blank sentences to work through assignments!

Using a Highlighter

If you own your textbooks or make notes on your own paper or handouts, you should be using a highlighter when you read and study for a subject. You've been practicing in this textbook by highlighting items for emphasis.

Although you can use a color that you prefer, yellow will not clutter a page or mark space in which you can take notes. Some readers use a second color to underline key words.

It can be a mistake to highlight everything on a page. You should always ask yourself what you are reading or studying for and begin with those concepts. **Other items you may want to highlight are:**

- Important words or concepts.
- Definitions
- Main ideas
- Steps in a process
- Ordered points (one, two, three)
- Quotations
- Quick points
- Summaries
- Conclusions

DON'T HIGHLIGHT:

- o Unimportant ideas
- o Questions
- o More than one example
- o Repeated items
- o Dialogue (unless it makes or supports a point)

Study Skill Practice: Highlight the following page carefully as you read.

Highlight Practice: "Why Do Adults Go to School?"

People return to educational setting for a variety of reasons. Cyril Houle, a researcher in **andragogy**, or the study of adult learning, designed a typology of adult learners which indicates most adult motivation falls within three categories:

Goal oriented. Adult learners who use education as a means of accomplishing fairly clear-cut objectives.

Activity oriented. Adult learners who find no connection between learning and a given educational activity.

Learning-oriented. Adult learners who seek knowledge for its own sake.

An example of each situation may include each of these case scenarios:

Goal oriented:
- o George returns to school to improve his job status.
- o Susan must get her GED to apply for a new job.
- o Mary wants to get her associate's in nursing.

Activity oriented:
- o Mr. Jones, a retired carpenter, attends class for interaction with other senior citizens.
- o LaTasha likes to make decorative household crafts.

Learning oriented.
- o Dr. Smith attends Russian language classes at NCCU.
- o A homeless high school grad attends basic skills math class.
- o Ms. White, a retired teacher, reads books on new teaching techniques.

As you read this information on motivation, did you consider which category you might fall under? In any case, your personal priorities and values will guide you as you pursue your college education.

Annotation

As you advance in note-taking and highlighting, you will begin to annotate your reading. What is **annotation**? It is written notes that the reader makes along the text's edges or margins as he or she interacts with or **study-reads** the materials. If you don't want to write in your book, (or just want to you're your notes "moveable") use sticky notes.

How do I annotate?
- o short words or phrases
- o symbols
- o abbreviations (any technique similarly used in note-taking)

What do I annotate?
- o important information
- o issues discussed
- o opinions or ideas

What do I note?
- o questions you have
- o info from lectures or other materials that are similar
- o definitions or info that clarifies

Look at the annotations for this part of Dr. King's "I Have a Dream" speech:

| The architects were slave owners! | In a sense we have come to our Nation's Capital to cash a check. When the architects of our great republic wrote the magnificent words of the Constitution and the Declaration of Independence, they were signing a promissory note to which every American was to fall heir. | Promissory? |

| See class note! | This note was a promise that all men, yes, black men as well as white men, would be guaranteed to the inalienable rights of life liberty and the pursuit of happiness. | What about women? |

Study Skill Activity: Now look at the following excerpt and **annotate** it! "Talk" to Dr. King's all-important speech on Civil Rights!

Dr. Martin Luther King, Jr.
"I HAVE A DREAM" SPEECH
August 28, 1963

I am happy to join with you today in what will go down in history as the greatest demonstration for freedom in the history of our nation.

Five score years ago, a great American, in whose symbolic shadow we stand today, signed the Emancipation Proclamation. This momentous decree came as a great beacon of hope to millions of slaves, who had been seared in the flames of whithering injustice. It came as a joyous daybreak to end the long night of their captivity. But one hundred years later, the colored America is still not free. One hundred years later, the life of the colored American is still sadly crippled by the manacle of segregation and the chains of discrimination.

One hundred years later, the colored American lives on a lonely island of poverty in the midst of a vast ocean of material prosperity. One hundred years later, the colored American is still languishing in the corners of American society and finds himself an exile in his own land So we have come here today to dramatize a shameful condition.

In a sense we have come to our Nation's Capital to cash a check. When the architects of our great republic wrote the magnificent words of the Constitution and the Declaration of Independence, they were signing a promissory note to which every American was to fall heir.

This note was a promise that all men, yes, black men as well as white men, would be guaranteed to the inalienable rights of life liberty and the pursuit of happiness.

It is obvious today that America has defaulted on this promissory note insofar as her citizens of color are concerned. Instead of honoring this sacred obligation, America has given its colored people a bad check, a check that has come back marked "insufficient funds."

But we refuse to believe that the bank of justice is bankrupt. We refuse to believe that there are insufficient funds in the great vaults of opportunity of this nation. So we have come to cash this check, a check that will give us upon demand the riches of freedom and security of justice.

We have also come to his hallowed spot to remind America of the fierce urgency of Now. This is not time to engage in the luxury of cooling off or to take the tranquilizing drug of gradualism.

Now is the time to make real the promise of democracy.
Now it the time to rise from the dark and desolate valley of segregation to the sunlit path of racial justice.
Now it the time to lift our nation from the quicksands of racial injustice to the solid rock of brotherhood.
Now is the time to make justice a reality to all of God's children.

I would be fatal for the nation to overlook the urgency of the moment and to underestimate the determination of it's colored citizens. This sweltering summer of the colored people's legitimate discontent will not pass until there is an invigorating autumn of freedom and equality. Nineteen sixty-three is not an end but a beginning. Those who hope that the colored Americans needed to blow off steam and will now be content will have a rude awakening if the nation returns to business as usual.

There will be neither rest nor tranquility in America until the colored citizen is granted his citizenship rights. The whirlwinds of revolt will continue to shake the foundations of our nation until the bright day of justice emerges.

We can never be satisfied as long as our bodies, heavy with the fatigue of travel, cannot gain lodging in the motels of the highways and the hotels of the cities.

We cannot be satisfied as long as the colored person's basic mobility is from a smaller ghetto to a larger one.

We can never be satisfied as long as our children are stripped of their selfhood and robbed of their dignity by signs stating "for white only."

We cannot be satisfied as long as a colored person in Mississippi cannot vote and a colored person in New York believes he has nothing for which to vote.

No, no we are not satisfied and we will not be satisfied until justice rolls down like waters and righteousness like a mighty stream.

I am not unmindful that some of you have come here out of your trials and tribulations. Some of you have come from areas where your quest for freedom left you battered by storms of persecutions and staggered by the winds of police brutality.

You have been the veterans of creative suffering. Continue to work with the faith that unearned suffering is redemptive.

Some Reading Techniques

There are many techniques for approaching your textbook reading assignments. Most importantly, remember you are **study-reading** as opposed to pleasure reading. Use this easy technique to get more out of your assignment. Use it in conjunction with highlighting and annotation. You've already been shown the SQ3R method in the introduction of this book; hopefully, you've tried to use in this text or in another course's readings this semester. Here are two more "techniques" that may help; the best one is the one that works for you!

ReQuest

The ReQuest method is a good drill technique to ensure success in gathering and synthesizing important **facts**, **definitions** and **main ideas** in a reading assignment.

STEPS:
o **Read** a passage silently or aloud at the same time as your partner (or a group).

o **Jot down** important **questions** about the reading that you think are important to know. Include why questions! (1 or 2 per paragraph).

o **Take turns asking and answering the questions.** <u>Note</u>: It is permitted to ask the same or similar questions to one another since this prepares the reader more fully to use and remember the information read.

Directed Reading Activity

Follow questions or ideas that an instructor gives you while you read a passage or chapter. Often study guides will give you this information, or the questions at the end of a chapter may direct you in your reading.

The questions you should be looking to answer are as follows:

1. What is the topic?
2. What does the author say about this topic?
3. Are there important dates, names, or definitions to be remembered?
4. Can I restate this concept or idea in my own words?
5. If I can't restate the main idea, what should I do?
6. Why is this information important? How does it fit in the "big picture"?

There is also help you can gain from your instructor. You may want to ask him or her to outline the following:

- What are we reading for?
- What important concepts should we look for?
- What definitions will be important?
- How will this information be tested or used (or what will be...)

Use these methods on the following passage or on a reading assignment in one of your textbooks.

Practice Reading: Andragogy and the Adult Learner

For many years education specialists centered their work and development around pedagogy or the science of helping children learn. Today adult educators practice *andragogy* or the science of helping adults learn. This "new" theory makes some basic assumptions about how adult learners are different from children.

Malcolm Knowles, the father of adult education, noted four basic characteristics about adult learners. First, an adult's self-concept moves from one of being a dependent personality towards one of being a self-directing human being. An adult has the ability to make choices and exercise freedoms. A man or woman determines the direction of his/her life and makes choices to meet his or her individual goals or needs.

A second assumption is that an adult accumulates a growing reservoir of experience that becomes an increasing resource for learning. A child's life experience is much more limited simply because he or she has not lived very long or had sufficient control of his or her life. An adult's life choices create experiences. These experiences include employment episodes, significant relationships, living arrangements, familial growth, and educational activity. An adult's life may be shaped by environment, people, personal history and physical health. All these shaping factors and life events are added to the wealth of an adult's learning because essentially all experiences are learning experiences!

A third characteristic of the adult learner involves his or her readiness to learn becomes oriented increasingly to the developmental tasks of his or her social roles. A young adult's role is that of becoming a responsible, productive part of society, so education will often be geared toward gainful employment and survival. A bit later, a young adult may become a parent, so he or she may see educational opportunities related to skillful parenting. As an adult ages, education may be sought to enhance a career, promote better health, prepare for future retirement or develop stress-relieving interests. A middle-aged adult, as part of the "sandwich" generation, may need education on how to deal with aging parents or grandparents and growing teenagers.

Finally the elder adult may need education as he or she faces imminent retirement which may include financial or health needs. For whatever stage an adult reaches, the educational needs are reflected.

Lastly, an adult learner's perception of time changes from one of eventual application of knowledge to the need to immediate application, and accordingly, his orientation toward learning shifts from one of subject centeredness to one of problem centeredness. A child learns to prepare for adulthood or some future career. An adult learner often needs to gain knowledge he or she can use immediately--to balance a checkbook, to gain a career move, to parent a troubled teen, etcetera. In kind, the adult's learning is centered around a problem he or she faces rather than learning a subject for a subject's sake. Writing is learned to write reports for a job or letters to creditors. If the information is not applicable, then an adult may not be as interested or eager to absorb it.

As Knowles defines andragogy, educators must become aware of the different needs of adults as programs are developed and curriculum is designed.

DRA Practice:

Excerpt from   THE BLACK EXPERIENCE IN AMERICA Published electronically by its author, Norman Coombs, and Project Gutenberg. (C 1993) by Norman Coombs

…The earliest written records were provided by the Arabs who developed close contact with West Africa by 800 A.D. After that, West Africans began using Arabic themselves to record their own history. In the middle of the fifteenth century, Europeans began regular contact with West Africa, and they left a wide variety of written sources. While most of these early Europeans were not men of learning, many of their records are still valuable to the student of history.

Ghana was already a powerful empire, with a highly complex political and social organization, when the Arabs reached it about 800 A,D. An Arabic map of 830 A.D. has Ghana marked on it, and other contemporary Arabic sources refer to Ghana as the land of gold. From this time on, a thriving trade developed between Ghana and the world of Islam, including the beginnings of a slave trade. However, this early slave trade was a two-way affair. Al-Bakri, a contemporary Arab writer, was impressed with the display of power and affluence of the Ghanaian king. According to him, the king had an army of two hundred thousand warriors which included about forty thousand men with bows and arrows. (Modern scholars know that the real power of the Ghanaian army was due not to its large numbers as much as to its iron- pointed spears.) Al-Bakri also described an official audience at the royal palace in which the king, the Ghana, was surrounded by lavish trappings of gold and silver and was attended by many pages, servants, large numbers of faithful officials, provincial rulers, and mayors of cities. On such occasions, the king heard the grievances of his people and passed judgment on them. Al- Bakri also describes lavish royal banquets which included a great deal of ceremonial ritual.

The Herringbone

One last study or reading technique is known as the Herringbone technique. This method is a way for the reader to identify the main idea of a passage or paragraph and the supporting details of that main idea. This method is similar to a web form where the main idea is listed in the middle circle and supporting details are written on attached sub-circles (see sample in appendix). These mind maps are particularly useful for visual and kinesthetic learners who may have trouble concentrating on long textbook chapters or reading passages.

HOW: Draw a fish skeleton like the one below. Write the main idea along the fish spine, then list supporting ideas on each of the ribs.

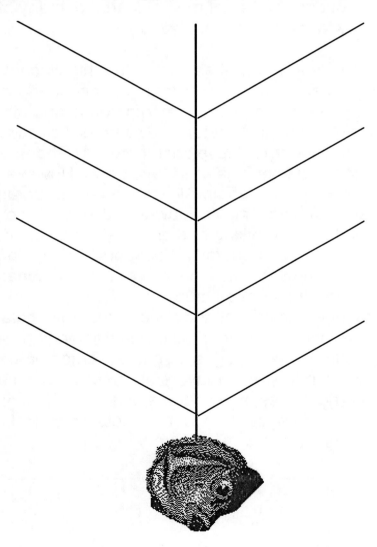

Mapping

This is a graphic organizer similar to the Herringbone. Put the central idea or thesis in the center and related ideas in the attached circles.

Note-taking

Note-taking is another fundamental component of academic success. It can be a difficult habit for some adult students to develop depending on whether they took notes (or chose not to) in high school. College instructors expect their students to take notes in class. Annotation is taking notes in your textbooks, but you also may need more detailed notes on paper. Even if you may not be used to taking notes in class, you should take notes for these and many other good reasons:

- Test preparation.
- Understanding key points in reading.
- Complement textbooks with additional information.
- Remember lectures or skills such as math.

Once you have notes how will you use them? There are several ways use notes:

- To prepare for tests or quizzes
- To develop paper or research ideas
- To remember key ideas or review skills
- To ask clarifying questions
- To answer worksheets or book exercises
- To focus and concentrate on lectures

Every time you take notes, you should include the following:

- ✓ Title or subject of lecture
- ✓ Date
- ✓ References to textbook pages
- ✓ Corresponding handouts or assignment sheets
- ✓ Definitions and key concepts
- ✓ Questions you may have

While there is no perfect way to take notes, following are some suggestions to get you started.

How to Take Notes

BEFORE YOU START:
- Use a 3-ring notebook.
- Divide pages with a recall column on the left. (See Cornell set-up)
- Arrive early and get your notebook out.
- Date each new day's notes.
- Number the pages and include either topic heading or chapter number at the top of the page.
- Prepare to listen. Make sure you're alert.
- Avoid distractions such as talking classmates, vibrating phones, or visual distractions such as windows

ARRANGEMENT Notes can be arranged in a variety of ways:

- comparison and contrast
- time order
- cause and effect
- problem and solution
- pros and cons
- steps in a method

Look at the sample page (in 2 pages) and decide which pattern of organization the taker used. How could you tell?

CLUES when to take notes:

- **Questions.** Write questions or problems proposed.
- **Notes on the board or screen.** Copy notes from the board or screen.
- **Listen for key words, steps or lists** such as first, second, or finally, next...
- **Watch the instructor for signals.** Listen closely if s/he uses slower speech, motions with hands, excited speech, or pauses.

Sample short symbols to use in note-taking:

Abbreviations:
- o gov. (government)
- o etc. (and so on)
- o educa. (education)
- o improv't (improvement)
- o ppl (people--leave out vowels)

Symbols:

∴ or =	therefore	@	at
/	with	?	question
×	not	· or →	(new point)
ø	not/without	! or ∗	(important concept)

Of course you can make up your own!

Use your *learning style* while you take notes. Note-taking may seem easier for the auditory or visual learner, but each style has its distractions, such as visual learners tend not to listen as well or auditory learners may not want to write things down. There are suggestions for utilizing your style on the following page.

Remember sticky notes from your annotation? Take them from your book and match them to your lecture notes!

How do I use my learning style to take notes?

Visual:
- o Use symbols
- o Use color pens/paper
- o Space notes to enhance later
- o Draw diagrams

Auditory:
- o Listen for key words
- o Sit near the front to hear every word
- o Ask clarifying questions or ask for repetition
- o Record the lecture

Kinesthetic:
- o Use comfortable writing instrument
- o Use a laptop computer or palm pilot
- o Draw symbols or icons next to key elements

Individual:
- o Sit near the front or at least from distracting groups
- o Write down questions to ask your instructor after class (you may feel more comfortable than asking in front of the group)

Group:
- o Sit away from distracting (sociable like you) students
- o Compare your notes with classmates

Reflection. What are your personal suggestions for note-taking?

SAMPLE NOTES PAGE

Islam
G. speaker/Ms Mut

3-10-98

→ Islam founded by prophet Muhamed
→ 600's in M. East
→ Koran
→ some more liberal today (Sunni)

what is jihad?

Islam	Chry
one god	one god
prophets	prophets/Christ
Koran	Bible
sects	denomination
worship/Fri.	worship/Sun

both Jerusalem as holy city?

→ women treated well
  — own property
  — husbands care for needs
  — divorce allowed
  — given "dowry"

→ other interesting pts
  — cover head/arms/legs (women)
  — pray facing east (Mecca)
  — Ramadan
  — take name of Mohamed

how convert?

→ 5 pillars
  1) one god/Mohamed
  2) alms
  3) pray 5x day

  4) fast Ramadan
  5) pilgrimage

SAMPLE NOTES PAGE

9-2-98

<u>Civil Rights Mov't</u>

<u>1950's</u>
→ Rosa Parks = bus boycott
in Montgomery, AL
→ Brown vs Topeka – school
board not segreg. students
S.Crt ruled "not equal"

<u>Leaders</u>

Martin L. King → peaceful approach
*1. Marches
2. sit-ins
3. boycotts

* March on Washington D.C.
Aug. '63
"<u>I Have a Dream</u>" Speech (see handout)
televised, ½ mil. people!

<u>Malcolm X</u>
→ Black Muslim
ask instructor! → Nation of Islam
→ more forceful, some believe
his approach meant violence

Cornell Note-taking Page Set-up

Draw a line 2 inches from edge for additional notes or to use as a recall column.

Lecture notes

Draw a line 3 inches from the bottom to add notes from your textbook. Or use sticky notes to take notes then move to this page.

What to Do <u>After</u> the Lecture

Taking notes can help you only if you use them later. Consider these suggestions to make the best use of your notes!

→ Review notes daily. Go over the previous class's notes before they grow cold. A few minutes every day will make studying for an exam much easier.

→ Take notes on your notes! Pull out key words or names and write these in the "Recall" column to the left.

→ Write questions on notes you still may not fully understand and ask these at the next class session.

→ Highlight your notes! Again, mark key words and information that may be more important after you've taken them.

→ Correlate notes to textbook information. Annotate your book and/or make correlating notes for your lecture notes.

→ Use the REQUEST method with a partner to study your notes.

→ Make study cards or use mnemonic devices to memorize essential information.

→ Use websites provided by your instructor or by the textbook's publisher or author. These may have exercises to reinforce your study or even practice tests to review.

Reflection:

1. What is difficult for you as you read or study your textbook? Is there a subject you particularly struggle with?

2. What note-taking strategies are you already using successfully?

3. What new note-taking strategy will you try? (Hint: ask another student to show you his or her notes.)

Critical Thinking

Critical thinking skills are those skills that go beyond simple reading for comprehension or facts. You should ask these kinds of questions when you read any information or material. These skills include:

analysis: Why did this happen?
application: How can I apply the information I'm reading?
synthesis: Could it be prevented or changed in some way?
inference: What is going on between the lines (beyond what I see)?

Following are some practices in critical thinking.

Analogies are used to compare the familiar with unfamiliar. Complete the following analogies:

1.   heart is blood as lungs are to _____

2.   Raleigh is to North Carolina as _____ is to state

3.   _____ is to liquid as ice is to solid

4.   hot is to cold as up is to _____

5.   man is to wife as _____ is to husband

6.   cashier is to cash register as bagger is to _____

7.   mowing is to summer as _____ is to winter

8.   shuttle is to _____ as an airplane is to atmosphere

9.   bank is to money as _____ is to milk

10.   happy is to joy as sad is to _____

11.   student is to failure as dieter is to _____

12.   seven is to forty-nine as nine is to _____

13.   camera is to photographer as highlighter is to _____

14.   associate's is to community college as bachelor's is to _____

15.   medicine is to disease as education is to _____

CRITICAL THINKING FUN

Look at the arrangement of the words, letters and/or numbers to decipher each phrase.

D ^{D} U ^{O} M ^{W} ^{n} P S	head heels	SOCK (in box)	R I rosie N G
NOON SUNDAY	88 KOAP	ccrrooss	PANTS PANTS
GNIKOOL	standing miss	EXXPOSURE	24 HIAD
1, 3, 4...38, 39, 40 LIFE	JOB IN JOB	HA	lal

If a plane crashes on the border of North and South Carolina, where would you bury the survivors?

Take two apples from three apples. How many apples do you have?

Answers in glossary

Some Questions to Think Critically About[5]

Would you accept $1,000,000 to quit school and never return?

If you found the answers to your course's final exam on a college copier what would you do?

If you knew there would be a nuclear war in one week, what would you do?*

Your house, containing everything you own, catches fire; after saving your loved ones and pets, you have time to safely make a final dash to save one item. What would it be?*

Your project is due tomorrow, but you receive a call that a close friend has been in an accident. How will you convince your instructor that you need more time to complete the work?

While parking late at night on campus, you slightly scrape the side of a Porsche. You are certain no one else is aware of what happened. The damage is minor and would not be covered by insurance. Would you leave a note?*

If you had to make a budget cut to save your program at the college, which would you cut: an instructor or a scholarship?

Given the ability to project yourself into the past but not return, would you do so? Where would you go? What would you try to accomplish if you knew you might change the course of history?*

An instructor assigns a six-page paper for your next class (which meets in two days). You have promised to keep your sister's child so she can go to work. What will you tell your sister in order to meet your class deadline?

---

[5] Starred questions adapted from The Book of Questions by Gregory Stock, Phd. (1985)

What the Students Say...

"I'm a visual learner, so I turn all of my notes into diagrams and pictures. This is especially useful in biology class because there is so much vocabulary to learn." (2009)

"I never took notes in high school, so I didn't even know what to write down in class. I started paying attention to the things the instructor repeated or wrote on the board. I always write down these things." (2008)

"Go to class and do what your instructor assigns... that's how to succeed here..." (2009)

Chapter 6

Test Taking and Memory Tips

Test Tips and Types
Preparing for the Test
Mnemonics
Test Anxiety
Testing Affirmations

Test Taking "Quiz"

See how savvy you are about taking tests with this true-false quiz. Read the following statements about test taking. Write TRUE or FALSE in the box next to each statement.

	1. On the day of the test, you should talk to as many other students as possible, especially students who have already taken the test.
	2. You should look around the room during the test to make sure that you aren't the last one to finish.
	3. You should ask your instructor for copies of old tests to use to study with.
	4. The mnemonic device "fanboys" (**f**or, **a**nd, **n**or, **b**ut, **o**r, **y**et, **s**o – coordinating conjunctions) is an acronym.
	5. You should write down any formulas or mnemonic devices on the test paper as soon as you get your paper.
	6. You should complete the test starting on page one and working through systematically.
	7. For every hour that you spend in class, you should study one hour out of class.
	8. You should begin studying for tests on the first day of class.
	9. If you have always been a poor test taker, you will always be a poor test taker.
	10. The words "never," "only," and "always" always make a true-false statement false.
	11. You should create a "cheat sheet" for every test.
	12. A student who studies five hours the night before an exam will make a better grade than a student who studies 45 minutes a day for five days.
	13. Students who suffer from test anxiety should cram for tests because their adrenaline will be so high, they will remember all of the material.
	14. You should always go with your first instinct. You should not change an answer unless you are positive that the second answer is correct.
	15. Students do not need to study for open-book tests.

Test Tips

Taking a test involves much more than studying a few facts and answering a few questions. In fact, you may already have encountered a variety of test questions in your education experiences. While studying and learning the material is your best preparation for testing, each type of question must be approached differently. Here is an overview of question types and some tips for answering each. Some hints on studying follows this section.

Multiple Choice Questions

A multiple choice question gives the tester several options to choose from. There is **no** maybe answer. The choice is simply right or wrong. Be wary of **distractors**; these are answers that are almost right but contain some small--perhaps not so obvious--error. Always check your choice, but when you are unsure, it often best to go with your first impulse. WARNING! NEVER leave a multiple choice question unanswered.

Tips:
- ❖ Be precise. Watch for **distractors**.
- ❖ Check your answer!
- ❖ Time your test questions (60 questions in one hour is one per minute!)
- ❖ Watch for answers that contain always, never, best, etc. There are usually no absolutes.
- ❖ Leave no question unanswered.
- ❖ Eliminate wrong choices to narrow down your possibilities.

SAMPLES: *Example answers in glossary*

1. The study method that requires reading, reviewing, and rereading is _____
   a. SQ3R   b. ReQuest   c. DRA   d. 3Rs

2. Malcolm Knowles said this study was different from adult learning.
   a. andragogy   b. pedagogy   c. pediatrics   d. animal

3. If you use SQ3R you will _____ important details.
   a. never learn   b. always learn   c. often remember   d. study fully

4. Reading techniques were designed for learners who_____
   a.   need to learn ways to avoid failure.   c.   want to become good readers.
   b.   want to develop good study habits   d.   want to become better learners.

True-False Questions

A true-false test requires you to read each statement and determine with it is right (true) or wrong (false). You have only two choices; therefore, you must read each statement carefully looking for any mistakes or flaws. One mistake or flaw makes the statement FALSE. Warning: watch for absolutes! Words such as always, never, best, or worst may mean the statement is **false**.

TIPS:
- ❖ Answer all true-false questions.
- ❖ Avoid absolute words.
- ❖ Look for any mistakes. The <u>whole</u> statement must be true.

SAMPLES: Mark each statement as true (T) or false (F).

____1.   The SQ3R method is a reading technique anyone can learn to use.
____2.   The SQ3R method is always effective for a social studies book.
____3.   The SQ3R method is better than the REQUEST method.
____4.   Previewing is not part of the SQ3R method.   *Answers in glossary*

Fill-in-the-Blank Questions

A fill-in-the-blank test is almost like a multiple choice test. The test may give you a **word bank** of possible answers you must use to fill in the missing blanks or you may have to remember the answers from your head. These answers are either right or wrong (unless the teacher chooses to give you credit for a synonym). Generally these questions are fact recall or definition questions.

TIPS:
- ❖ Try to fill in **every** blank, especially when you're given choices.
- ❖ Mark off choices.
- ❖ Check over the test for clues to answers.
- ❖ Skip ones you do not know and answer those you do first.

SAMPLES:

A _____ test may give you a word bank to use.

The first step in SQ3R method is _____.

You should try to fill in _____ blank on the test!

Short Answer Questions

A short answer test is simply that. You must write out short answers (sentences may be required) to explain definitions or questions. Generally, a few sentences are required. Make sure you include all the information asked for (dates, places, names, why it's important, etc.).

Tips:

❖ Write down something for each item. You may receive partial credit.
❖ Study for short answers test with short answer notes.
❖ Look over your test for other hints to answers.
❖ Don't repeat yourself.
❖ If you have choices, ask if you can do more than required.

SAMPLE:

Directions: Choose 2 items and explain what each is and why it is important.

SQ3R   Paraphrasing   Fact vs Opinion   Planner

Essay Questions

Of all the types of questions, the essay is the most subjective, that is it will be graded by what the teacher is looking for or thinks is correct. It may include both fact and opinion. The question may ask you to analyze or apply the information you have learned. You will be asked to write one or more paragraphs. Make sure you include the most important idea and details to back it up! Study a variety of facts to prepare for such tests!

TIPS:

❖ Use complete sentences.
❖ Read the question at least TWICE before you answer it.
❖ Make a short outline (list) of what you will write.
❖ Save the most time for essay questions since they usually count the most.

SAMPLE:

Explain the SQ3R method of reading. Compare it to one other method.

Open-Book Tests

Some instructors choose to give tests known as "open-book" tests. Students should never think that these tests are easier or that there is no need to study. In fact, this type of test can give the instructor a chance to see how much the student has synthesized and incorporated the information for the course.

Questions tend to be essay or short answer, and the student's answers should be quite detailed with information from lectures, books, labs and even additional research. If given out-of-class, then plan the same time you would have used to study for an in-class exam. If given in class, then study your notes and texts, so you will have plenty of time to find the answers in the limited class time.

Finally, review your answers carefully for organization, complete sentences, and correct grammar and spelling.

Tests on Learning Management (Computer) Systems

Be aware that these delivery methods can have the same kind of test questions as a pencil and paper test. However, there are some additional things to watch for:

- o **Deadlines**. Has the instructor set a deadline for the test to be taken? If so, plan carefully to prepare and take the test just like you would for one in class.

- o **Time-limits.** An instructor may set the program to run a set amount of time. Read instructions carefully for this and plan. The program will end your test at the time limit set.

- o **Force Completion.** Test may not allow the test taker to go back to a previous question once the answer is submitted.

- o **Submit carefully**. Make sure you follow the instructions carefully by submitting and/or saving each and every answer.

Oral Tests

Occasionally, you will be required to take an oral or verbal test. Most commonly, these kinds of tests are given in a foreign language or speech class. However, these tests may be given in other settings such as a nursing class or other course where the instructor is looking for mastery in the material as demonstrated in this form.

Performance Tests

In some courses, the student is taught to perform specific tasks such as engine or computer repair. In a clinical style class, the student may need to work with patients or complete step-by-step procedures. The best way to practice for this kind of test is to go to a lab or setting where you can manipulate the materials you will be tested on. In many cases, these tests are vital to the student's mastery of skills.

Standardized Tests

Tests for licensure or given by testing companies have strict rules. Make sure you listen to your proctor (an administrator who watches test takers complete exams) carefully!

- ☐ Make sure you have an appointment and paid (if required) any test fees.
- ☐ Arrive <u>early</u> with all necessary documents and identification.
- ☐ Do not bring food or drink.
- ☐ Leave your cell phone at home or off! If it rings, you will be asked to leave and forfeit your test.
- ☐ If you are ill, try to re-schedule. But NEVER just not show up! You forfeit test fees and may be denied a timely new test date.
- ☐ Relax. Take quiet deep breaths and follow the earlier test tips!

Reflection:

1. What do you need to improve about your test-taking skills?

2. What do you typically do in order to prepare? (Answer then read further!)

Studying for Tests

Preparing for a test should not be the anxiety-ridden, heart-wrenching, or time-consuming event it's often made out to be. If you have completed assignments all along and reviewed notes at least weekly, then you should have a lot of skills tuned for your next test.

Here are some tips for preparing for that BIG ONE.

A WEEK OR MORE BEFORE:

1. Don't cram the night before.
2. Start at least a week ahead of time. Schedule extra study time. Mark it out on your calendar. Make it a PRIORITY.
3. Review class notes.
4. Prepare your study guide.
5. Review your highlighted readings in textbooks. Don't just reread. After a few sections or pages, recite aloud or jot down the main points you just covered.
6. Avoid distractions--housework always looks good before a test.
7. Study with a classmate or friend.
8. Practice math and writing skills.
9. Make up some sample questions of your own.
10. Relax. Reward yourself after several hours of study.

THE NIGHT BEFORE:

1. DON'T CRAM.
2. Get a good night's rest before the big test.
3. Review your notes briefly, especially items you've had trouble with.

THE DAY OF THE TEST

1. Eat a good meal. If caffeine bothers you, avoid it.
2. Make sure you have all your needed tools: pens, pencils, calculators, exam booklets. Take extra pencils; sharpen them before the test.
3. Arrive early. Being late distracts others, makes you rushed and may even prevent your entry. (Some instructors don't admit late testers!)

4. Turn off your cell phone! Put it away, so its vibration doesn't distract you.
5. Look over the WHOLE test and map out your time. (Remember: spend the most time on items that count the most).
6. Do the questions you know first and go back to the harder ones. (Remember to spend time on those with the most points.)
7. Review. Go over your test and check for mistakes. Proofread any answers you wrote out. Check math problems.

SOME "FINAL" TIPS

✓ Ask instructors for sample or practice tests. Some departments have copies of old tests students can look at.

✓ Make up some of your own questions; especially look at textbook questions which is where instructors often get their questions!

✓ Use the REQUEST reading technique with another student to practice questions.

✓ Always remember, the first test is a "feel-out" test where you get a sense of how an instructor tests. Don't be afraid to ask the instructor to go over your results with you.

TESTING CENTERS

Your campus most likely has a formal testing center to administer standardized and licensure tests. Follow their rules strictly and arrive on time prepared and ready to go. Some instructors may use the testing center or learning lab/center for make-up testing, but ALWAYS check ahead of time because some college instructors have a strict NO MAKEUP policy.

Memorization Techniques

Mnemonics is the study of memory and how people bring information from the short term memory into the long-term memory. The long-term memory is what will help someone in his/her career activities. This information can be learned just from practice, but there are basic facts that must be embedded in your memory storage. No matter how much you try to avoid memorizing, there some things best suited for memorizing.

- ❖ Math facts.
- ❖ Math formulas.
- ❖ Weights and measures.
- ❖ Dates for history.
- ❖ Grammar rules.
- ❖ Names of important characters or historical figures.
- ❖ Science definitions.
- ❖ Spelling or vocabulary words.
- ❖ Steps in a process.

How do I memorize? Here are some tips:

Make flashcards.

Keep them where you sit often or carry them in your notebook. Take them out and review them often (daily) until you know them.

Use Repetition.

- ❖ Say facts aloud again and again.
- ❖ Drill them to a friend.
- ❖ Write down facts or words over and over.
- ❖ Find a website that drills you—there are a lot!

(more tips on next page)

Create or find a mnemonic aid (such as an acrostic sentence).

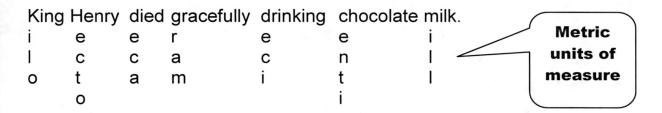

King Henry died gracefully drinking chocolate milk.

King	Henry	died	gracefully	drinking	chocolate	milk.
i	e	e	r	e	e	i
l	c	c	a	c	n	l
o	t	a	m	i	t	l
	o				i	

Metric units of measure

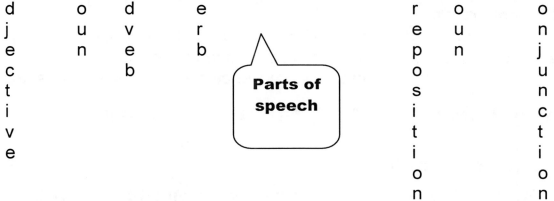

Anxious Noah actually verbalized, "<u>Interjections!</u>" past no one because he could.

Anxious	Noah	actually	verbalized,	"Interjections!"	past	no		because			he could.
d	o	d	e		p	o		o
j	u	v	r		r	u		n
e	n	e	b		e	n		j
c		b			p			u
t					o			n
i					s			c
v					i			t
e					t			i
					i			o
					o			n
					n			

Parts of speech

Loci Method. Make up a story or use locations you are familiar with.

Imagine your information in different places in your home or room, then make up a story using the information you need to remember.

Use acronyms.

HOMES: Huron, Ontario, Michigan, Erie, Superior (Great Lakes)
FANBOYS: for, and, nor, but, or, yet, so (conjunctions)

Make a rhyme.

In 1492, Columbus sailed the ocean blue.
"I" before "e" except after "c" or when sounds like "a" as in neighbor or weigh.

Add music.

Rap or sing a series of items you need to know.

Organize info into chunks.

For instance, instead of memorizing 50 states, organize them according to geographical sections.

Tap into your learning style:
* Use things you touch if you're kinesthetic. (Try slick paper or cardboard)
* Use I-pod recordings or DVDs if you're oral or auditory.
* Use pictures or colorful pens if you're visual.
* Highlighters are great for visual or kinesthetic.
* Sticky notes tap into all three: they're bright colors; you can move them around; you can say what's on each as you move them.

Check the Internet!

There are lots of presentations on YouTube and other websites designed to help students memorize specialized information such as medical terms and human anatomy or science and math steps or facts.

Last but not Least: PRACTICE, PRACTICE, PRACTICE!

Memorization Activity:

Instructions: Memorize each greeting for "Hello" and the country in which it's used.

Country	In Language	Pronunciation
Mexico	"Hola!"	oh-la
France	"Bonjour"	bone-jur
Italy	"Buon giorno"	bwohn JOR-noh
Germany	"Guten Tag"	gooten-tog
China	"Ni hao"	Nee HaOW
Japan	"Konnichiwa"	Ko-nee-chee-wah
Greece	"Kalimera"	Kah-lee-MEH-rah
Russia	"Zdravstvuite"	ZzDRAST-vet-yah
Israel	"Shalom"	Shah-lohm
Hawaii	"Aloha"	Ah-loh-hah

Test Anxiety

Do you suffer from any of the following symptoms just prior to a test?

- ☐ Nausea
- ☐ Nervous nail chewing, twitching, finger tapping.
- ☐ Sweaty palms
- ☐ Rapid heartbeat
- ☐ Inability to sleep the night before
- ☐ Use of excuses to miss the test

If you answered "yes" to one or more of the above, then you suffer from **test anxiety**. Some people get anxiety because they failed to schedule study time and prepare for the test. Others have an involuntary response to tests and suffer anxiety.

If you get test anxiety involuntarily, then you need to learn to force yourself to face the test--don't run away. If you don't do well, tell your instructor, so he or she may be able to make suggestions to help. You may also want to use the following affirmations to prepare and clear your mind before and during tests.

Special Note: If you had special accommodations in public school (often called an "IEP"), go to your college counseling office and have them prepare an accommodations plan for your college work. This can include extra time or a special environment for testing!

Testing Affirmations

Use these to prepare yourself mentally for testing. Take a deep breath, then say each to yourself several times.

👍 I have studied for this test. I know the material. I am sure I can do this test!

👍 I am an excellent student. I have worked hard. I will do well on this test!

👍 I know the words. I know the concepts. I have prepared for this. I will be successful!

👍 Tests are my life! I live for tests! I can't wait for this test! I am ready!

👍 There are no bad tests!

👍 Beware tests! The master test-taker is here!

👍 This test is mine!

Reflection: Think about other affirmations you have used. How did they make you feel? Now write your own testing or student affirmation.

Practicum and Scenarios

Read the following scenarios and make a suggestion to help each student overcome his/her study or testing difficulty.

1. Sara has two midterm tests tomorrow. She has had difficulty in the Calculus class and is not sure about how to do all the problems. She made only a 70 on the last English 111 test she took. What do you advise Sara to do?

2. Tom has a computer test next week when he will have to write several formulas for MS Excel. This is not his strongest computer skill. What do you advise Tom to do?

3. Lila has an oral exam in Spanish in two weeks. She often "freezes" when she has to speak in front of others. She will be given a topic next week to prepare for her exam. What should Lila do?

4. Monty has severe test anxiety. On his last exam, he completely "blanked out" and took nearly 30 minutes to remember what the class had just covered for this exam. What should Monty do during his exam tomorrow?

5. In Biology 165, Bebe has to memorize the body systems of humans for the exam in three weeks. There will be diagrams to label and multiple choice questions. How should Bebe prepare?

6. In order to be accepted into the Nursing program, Steve must learn all the equipment in a typical intensive care patient room. He must demonstrate this to the nursing instructor and get at least 90% of the items correct. What do you advise Steve to do?

What the Students Say...

Well today is test day…I think test anxiety is a major obstacle for me and my grades. Breathing is going to help and being prepared is good. AN (2008)

I usually adhere to a pre-test ritual. If I can, I get off work early…When I get home I review any problem areas…lasts about 15-20 minutes. After that I take a shower …find something comfortable to wear… have a light snack… and arrive 20-30 minutes early, so I don't feel rushed… doesn't guarantee a good grade… puts me in a pretty good mood. MS (2008)

I don't worry about tests… I took notes… I read the text… (2008)

..to lower my anxiety about taking tests is to study. I study with either classical music or jazz music playing. JJ (2008)

Appendix A: Research Techniques

Additional information to help students on writing assignments.

Introduction to the Research Paper

Colleges and universities are all about the research. Instructors and professors have engaged in large amounts of it to earn their credentials. Most continue in doing research as they teach your courses. So, it is an expectation or skill that every student must master, but this is much more than clicking on your Google search engine.

Most often, the most important part of this work is the PROCESS. Writing the paper will be much easier if you follow these steps!

The steps to doing a research paper are:

1. Choosing a topic.
2. Forming questions about the topic.
3. Researching the topic.
4. Making note-cards.
5. Organizing the notes into an outline.
6. Rough Draft.
7. Proofreading—both on the computer and a hard copy!
8. The Final Draft.
9. The Bibliography.
10. One final proofreading!

Get to know your library and enjoy the new information you are about to find!

Reference Materials
A Glossary

Following is a list of reference materials you may use when doing research. It is not an exhaustive list; therefore, ask your librarian for help!

Dictionary

A reference book containing an alphabetical list of words, with information given for each word, usually including meaning, pronunciation, and etymology.

Thesaurus

A book of synonyms, often including related and contrasting words and antonyms.

Encyclopedia

A comprehensive reference work containing articles on a wide range of subjects or on numerous aspects of a particular field, usually arranged alphabetically.

Abstract

A book of statements summarizing the important points of texts that are published on a topic or field of study.

Online card catalogue

A list or itemized display, as of titles, reference materials, magazines, journals, or articles in a library, usually including descriptive information of the material's contents. Books or magazines may be listed by author, subject or title. Most catalogues are now computerized.

Indexes

Something that serves to guide, point out, or otherwise facilitate reference, especially an alphabetized list of names, places, and subjects treated in a printed work, giving the page or pages on which each item is mentioned. An index may also be a book of titles on a particular subject or field of study.

Atlas

A book or bound collection of maps, sometimes with supplementary illustrations and graphic analyses.

Almanac

An annual publication including calendars with weather forecasts, astronomical information, tide tables, and other related tabular information. The annual publication composed of various lists, charts, and tables of information in one field or many unrelated fields.

Fiction

A literary work whose content is produced by the imagination and is not necessarily based on fact. The category of literature comprising works of this kind, including novels and short stories.

Non-fiction

A book or published work based on true facts. It simply reports facts or history or science. Many magazines and journals are nonfiction.

Biography

An account of a person's life written, composed, or produced by another. (An **auto**biography is written by the subject).

Reference book

A source of information such as an encyclopedia or almanac. Generally, these cannot be checked out of a library.

Bibliography

The description and identification of the editions, dates of issue, authorship, and typography of books or other written material. A compilation of such information at the end of a research paper, article or book.

Cross-reference

A reference to another part of a book or another source of information on the same subject.

Library of Congress System

College libraries use an alphabetical system based on topic areas to file their books. Check with your librarian about how books are shelved. (see page 190 for more information)

the Internet

The Internet or World Wide Web can be a source of information, but beware of sites that post information that is merely someone's ideas or opinions. Look for sites associated with museums (.org), government (.gov), research facilities (.org), schools, colleges or universities (.edu). Use a search engine to find information. A section on using search engines is located in the computer research appendix.

Databases

Most colleges subscribe to a series of databases that provide professional journal articles and research valuable to the college research process. Some may be specialized such as the INFOTRAC Health Reference Center (for nurses or med-techs) or Westlaw Primary (for legal research).

Net Library or E-books

Many community college libraries are small compared to a university, so they all subscribe to an online service to provide electronic versions of books. However, just like library books they cannot be accessed by more than one person at a time or more than one page at a time.

Reserve Desk

Located in the library, it is a place where your instructor may have specialized books or videos for your use in research. These materials cannot be checked out, but are used in the library. Bring your college ID or library card (which is usually your college ID). Bring change to make copies if necessary!

Activity: Visit a library and locate each item. Browse through the book stacks and locate card or computer catalogues.

Where to Look

Libraries, Bookstores & More

Whether you've chosen a topic or are still looking, there are several places you can go. These physical locations have books and materials that may not be as overwhelming as the Internet. They also have many sources that are NOT on the web which means they may be more current or professional in scope and coverage.

The library

Go to the college library or a local public library. Often college libraries have much more material and a computerized card catalogue. They also pay for scholarly databases which provide specific collegiate research. Some colleges require that you be a student to use them or check out materials, while universities allow use but no checkout for non-students. Bring your student ID card, so you can check materials out. Most libraries have a copier, so bring some change!

Your college library is organized by the **Library of Congress System**. The call letters are organized by subject, then by author. Once you've located the subject area (and it will be very detailed such as science then by subdivisions such as *chemistry* then *organic chemistry* and so forth).

Here is a general listing of subjects:

A:	General Works (including newspapers, magazines, etc)	M:	Music
		N:	Fine Arts
B:	Philosophy, Psychology and Religion	P:	Language and Literature
C:	Sciences of History	Q:	Science
D:	World History (other than Americas)		
E-F:	History of the Americas	R:	Medicine
G:	Geography	S:	Agriculture
H:	Social Sciences	T:	Technology
J:	Political Science	U:	Military Science
K:	Law	V:	Naval Science
L:	Education	Z:	Library Science

To read the CALL NUMBER, look at the following for the book titled, *Emergency Nursing Secrets*, by Kathleen Oman.

RT 120.E4 E484 2007

R refers to the subject of medicine and T is the subdivision for nursing. The rest is the number given to this book. Some books in the library are located in a section known as the REFERENCE section; although the books are still classified by the LC, they are not available for check-out. The reference books are usually in high demand, such as dictionaries or criticism series, so they must be available to all students or library users.

Ask the librarian for help, since it his/her duty to serve patrons. Respect the use of the library by others by remaining quiet and waiting your turn. Return materials to proper places. (**Note**: most libraries have a return cart to assure materials are replaced properly.)

Bookstores

A bookstore can be a wealth of information especially for more recently-published books and magazines. Bookstores are organized by subject, then each shelf is alphabetized. Used bookstores may not be as organized, but the books are cheap and the help usually friendly. Use the bookstore to research topic ideas and look for books to see in the library!

More places...

The media can be an important source of information. Local newspapers have archives. You may be able to talk to the reporter of a special article. The local television and radio stations may have people you can interview. Museums may have libraries or brochures. A tour can yield a great deal of information.

The phone book (online or actual paper) is a source you have at home. Check for agencies that serve the public. There may be a resource line sponsored by the newspaper or the agriculture department. Most government agencies have free brochures and pamphlets which can be used in research. Check the tourist bureau or an information office at a local college, town hall, or major company.

The Internet

The world-wide web has provided a seemingly unending source of information, but be aware for every reliable source, there are hundreds of unreliable sources. Websites marked as .edu, .org, or .gov are generally more professional and provide *researched* information. For academically appropriate work, you must use professionally-researched material. Use the MLA or APA citation. See your library for the format style used in your classes. Confirm this by checking with your instructor since both may be used at your college. You must cite sources in order to give credit for other people's work and research; not citing sources is considered PLAGIARISM, a serious violation of academic honesty. Ask for help if you are unsure how to provide correct citations in your papers and assignments. This includes both written and electronic documents (such as Powerpoint).

Explanations of how to cite sources and create bibliographies (a list of cited sources) follow. Try the following activities and scavenger hunts to hone your research skills!

Activity: (Choose three)

_____Visit a bookstore and find **ten** books on a subject of interest.
_____Call and interview one member of the media on a current issue.
_____Find three government or public agencies you can call.
_____Pick up four pamphlets or guides on your home town.
_____Find a free newspaper you can use for research.
_____Go to YouTube.com and do a search on current event; watch the
        video and think of how you use the information.

College Scavenger Hunt

Look at your college's catalogue (paper or online) to find out the following information about resources that will help you become successful.

1. Find a map of your campus and locate the following departments or people. Fill in the name of any person:

Person or Department	Building	Room
Your Advisor		
Your College President		
This course's instructor		
Your program's department		
Library		
Security		
Admissions		
Career Counseling		
Academic Counseling		
Transfer Center (if different from above)		
Financial Aid		
Tutoring		

2. Where are two open labs you can use for doing papers or online work?
3. Where can you get tutoring on campus? Write down where and times available. Note if there are specific subject areas you can get tutoring in.
4. What is your student governing body called? What do they do for the student body? When do they meet?
5. Write down the names of three student organizations (or clubs). Choose ones that would be beneficial to you.
6. How much is tuition for one credit hour at your college? How much would it cost for 12 credit hours. Are there any fees?
7. What are student fees used for?
8. What are the Main Campus library's hours of operation this semester?
9. What does a student need to have in order to use a textbook on reserve in the library?
10. How much do photocopies cost in the library?
11. What is the last date for withdrawing from a class this semester?
12. What are three things you should do in order to pre-register for the next semester?

Scavenger Hunt A

Go to the library and find answers to each of the following questions. Write down a source for each answer. Use the bibliography guide for form.

1. Name four newspapers of large metropolitan areas (Population over 300,000).
2. What year did Jesse Owens when an Olympic medal for a track event?
3. How many times has Jesse Jackson tried for a presidential or vice-presidential nomination?
4. How many Oscar nominations did *The Color Purple* receive? Who directed the movie? Who penned the novel?
5. What is the longitude and latitude of the big island of Hawaii?
6. To what country was Shirley Temple Black an ambassador?
7. What does "jihad" mean?
8. What is the origin of the word "barbarian"?
9. What is the "New Age Movement"?
10. In what year(s) did Jack the Ripper kill his victims? Where did these killings occur?
11. In what play did the character "Prospero" appear?
12. Where would a battered woman go for help locally? (Name 2 places that are not the police or hospital)
13. What was the first capitol of North Carolina?
14. What does the word "secede" mean? Who did it in 1860?
15. "Who wrote *The Origin of Species*, and what theory does it support?
16. What is the albedo of the Earth?
17. How many inches of rain does North Carolina average in one year?
18. What is the average number of people kill by lightning in North Carolina? In auto accidents?
19. What is the Bradley method of childbirth?
20. Name three colleges that have a hazard-waste management field or major.
21. In what year was the newspaper, *News and Observer*, founded?
22. Name three men who have set foot on the moon.
23. Name three Native American nations native to the South.
24. How many calories need to be used to lose one pound of fat?
25. How many community colleges are there in North Carolina?

Bonus: In what war, did more Americans die than any other? How many?

Scavenger Hunt B

Go to the library and find answers to each of the following questions. **Write down a source for each answer.** Use the bibliography guide for form.

1. Name four professional journals.
2. Name two African-American writers from the 1950s. Name one piece of work for each.
3. How many times has Robert Dole run for president ?
4. How many Oscars did *Philadelphia* receive? Who directed the movie?
5. What is the longitude and latitude of the island of Okinawa?
6. Who negotiated peace talks during the Vietnam War?
7. Where did spaghetti originate? Who brought it to Europe?
8. What is the origin of the word "radar"?
9. What is "Humanism"?
10. Name three countries that have capital punishment.
11. In what sixteenth century play did the character "Cordelia" appear?
12. Where would a homeless individual go for help locally? (Name 2 places that are not the police or hospital.)
13. Who donated land for the current capitol of North Carolina?
14. What does the word "transubstantiation" mean? With what institution is this connected?
15. Who wrote *The Communist Manifesto*? In what year?
16. What is the albedo of Venus?
17. How many inches of rain does Greensboro, NC, average in one year?
18. What is the average number of people killed by drowning in North Carolina? In train accidents?
19. What does La Leche League support? Find the number of a local chapter.
20. Name three colleges that have a nuclear engineering degree.
21. In what year was the newspaper, *The Independent,* founded?
22. Name three men who have commanded a shuttle mission.
23. Name three Native American nations native to the Southwest.
24. Name the first African-American president of a North Carolina community college. How many community colleges are there in North Carolina?
25. Name three women activists from the 1960s.

Bonus: Who said, "I have nothing to give but blood, toil and tears"?

© 2010, J.R. Stuart

Scavenger Hunt C

Go to the library and find answers to each of the following questions. **Write down a source for each answer.** Use the bibliography guide for form.

1. Name four professional journals.
2. Name two women writers from the1950s. Name one piece of work for each.
3. For what state was Sonny Bono representative?
4. How many Oscars did *Jurassic Park* receive? Who directed the movie?
5. What is the longitude and latitude of the island of Puerto Rico?
6. Name two American Civil War generals for the North and two for the South.
7. Where did spaghetti originate? Who brought it to Europe?
8. What is the origin of the word, "mafia"?
9. What is "Humanism"?
10. Name three countries that whose primary religion is Islam.
11. Name three African-American activists from the 1960s (not Malcolm X or MLK).
12. Where would a homeless individual go for help locally? (Name 2 places that are not the police or hospital)
13. Name 3 cities that have served as capitol of North Carolina.
14. What does the word "transubstantiation" mean? With what institution is this connected?
15. Who wrote the political pamphlet, *Common Sense*? In what year?
16. Which former planet may be a binary?
17. How many inches of rain does Wilmington, NC, average in one year?
18. What is the average number of people killed in farm-related accidents in North Carolina? In traffic accidents?
19. What does Habitat for Humanity support? Find the number of a local chapter.
20. Name three colleges or universities that have a marine biology degree.
21. In what year was the newspaper, *News and Observer,* founded?
22. Name a woman who has piloted a shuttle mission.
23. Name three Native American nations native to Eastern states.
24. Name the first African-American president of a North Carolina community college. How many community colleges are there in North Carolina?
25. In what nineteenth century play did the character "Earnest" appear?

Bonus: Who said, "We must learn to live together as brothers or perish together as fools"?

The Next Step
Asking the Right Questions

Once you have a topic, you need to begin your research. Follow these easy steps to begin.

1. Read about your topic in the encyclopedia or selected Internet sites such as Wikipedia.

2. Find a current magazine article on the topic (if possible).

3. Jot down the background or definitions of your topic.

4. Write down three or four questions you want to answer. Suggested questions:

    o What is the background of _____?
    o Why is this important?
    o What are the controversial points?
    o What is being done (or was done)?
    o Who are the main players or places involved?
    o What are the solutions?

5. Now make a note of WHERE you're going to look for the answers. Again, remember that not all research can be Internet based.

Research Note-cards

Note-cards on your research are important since this is where you'll write down what you find. They're convenient since you can organize them by simply shuffling the order!

You can make the notes in a variety of ways, but you should put the author or book title on each card in a set. (One set per book or article.) The first card you make you should have just the bibliography information. Here is an example:

John Vesilund
"The Sonoran Desert"
National Geographic
June, 1993   Vol. XX,
Number 6

The **full reference** of the article used is noted. It is helpful to write the author's name or book title on several cards before you begin to take notes. Now look at the notes taken on a card (next page).

Notice that:

- The notes are **not** in complete sentences.
- A topic heading is on the first line.
- The author's name (or website) and page number are at the top (this is very important when you organize cards later).

Sonoran Desert--native plants	Vesilind
saguaros-huge cacti	
native herbs--used for healing	
farm crops--chili peppers	
horses and cattle--raised by cowboys	

You should note that you should stay on topic for each card. If you see an interesting idea, then start a new card! Put as much or little as you want, but use your own words which will prevent plagiarism (copying of someone's words). If you copy, use quotation marks!

Study Skills Activity:

Go to the article, "Andragogy and the Adult Learner," in Chapter 5 and make several note-cards on it. How would you write the reference for it?

Doing a Bibliography

A bibliography is list of books, pamphlets, magazine articles and othe resources used in research. Generally this is found at the end of a researcl paper, a book or magazine article. An *annotated* bibliography is one that has notes about how that source could be useful for a chosen topic.

The information is listed the same for each item used, then the list is alphabetized. The easiest way to do a bibliography is to organize the note-cards with titles on them. In the samples below, follow all punctuation marks. Capitalize names and titles. Ask your instructor about the form he or she requires (MLA or APA). The MLA form is:

Books.

LAST NAME OF AUTHOR, FIRST NAME OF AUTHOR. TITLE OF BOOK. (PLACE OF PUBLICATION: PUBLISHER). DATE.

Magazine article.

LAST NAME OF AUTHOR, FIRST NAME OF AUTHOR. "TITLE OF MAGAZINE ARTICLE." TITLE OF MAGAZINE. VOLUME. NUMBER. DATE.

Book without author.

TITLE OF BOOK. (PLACE OF PUBLICATION: PUBLISHER). DATE.

Magazine article without author.

 "TITLE OF MAGAZINE ARTICLE." TITLE OF MAGAZINE. VOLUME. NUMBER. DATE.

Pamphlet or flyer.

TITLE OF PAMPHLET OR FLYER. (PLACE OF PUBLICATION: PUBLISHER). DATE.

Internet or World Wide Web

NAME OF SITE. DATE. WEB ADDRESS.

FINDING THE INFORMATION

✓ For a book, look at the first three pages.

✓ The copyright © date is the publication date.

✓ In a magazine, check the front of the magazine for volume, number and date. The title of the article is on the first page of the article. The author may be listed with the title or the very end of the article.

✓ Encyclopedia articles are listed just like magazines!

✓ Always check the <HOME> page of a website for the name of the website and possible authors. Use URL address at the top of your Internet browser window.

When do I cite a source?

✓ All dates, numbers and statistics!

✓ Direct quotations in quotation marks.

✓ Definitions or specific jargon

✓ Pictures you copy from the Internet!

✓ Any literature directly recited.

✓ Word-for-word verbal quotations (live or recorded).

Remember: Avoid "cut and paste" items!

Practice: Write each entry in correct order and alphabetize all.

A Bibliography on Literacy

Daniel D. Pratt authored "Tutoring Adults: Toward A Definition of Tutorial Role and Function in Adult Basic Education" in *Adult Literacy and Basic Education*, Volume 7 and Number 3 in 1983.

"Making Adult Basic Education Work: A Change in Emphasis" in the *NASSP Bulletin*, Volume 67, November 1983 by Richard W. Lane.

Angelica W. Cass wrote *Basic Education for Adults* which was published by Association Press in New York.

"ABE/GED Teachers: Characteristics and Training Needs by Kay Camperell and John Rachal and W. Lee Pierce Volume 7. Number 2, 1983 of the journal of *Adult Literacy and Basic Education*

Helping Adults Learn by Alan B. Knox published by Jossey-Bass Publishers in San Francisco in 1986.

Gary J. Conti wrote "The Principles of Adult Learning Scale" in *Adult Literacy and Basic Education* which came out in the spring of 1982.

Last Gamble on Education: Dynamics of Adult Basic Education was written by Jack Mezirow, Gordon Darkenwald and Alan Knox which was published in Washington by the Adult Education Association of the U.S.A. in 1975.

National Institute on Literacy provides information from federal departments such as the Department of Education (http://www.nifl.gov/)

Paper Writing
Topic Sentences/ Thesis Statement

Winston Churchill outlined the basic essay by saying:

    ✓Tell them what you're going to tell them.   **(Introduction)**
    ✓Then tell them.   **(Supporting)**
    ✓Finally, tell them what you told them.   **(Conclusion)**

When writing your essay, follow these steps:

*1. **ALWAYS BEGIN YOUR PAPER WITH AN INTRODUCTORY PARAGRAPH.** This Paragraph will include an introduction to your topic idea and your THESIS STATEMENT. The thesis statement is your topic sentence for the PAPER. In a standard paper, you will list all your topic headings in the thesis statement.

EXAMPLE: There are generally three types of recycling a typical household must deal with: paper, glass and plastic.

EXAMPLE: I enjoy vacationing in the mountains, on the coast, and in Washington, D.C.

*2. **INCLUDE YOUR DETAILS IN YOUR SUPPORTING PARAGRAPHS.** Each paragraph after the introduction are the topics expanded into supporting details. Each PARAGRAPH SHOULD BEGIN WITH YOUR TOPIC SENTENCE. Your topic sentence tells your reader what will be discussed in that paragraph.

EXAMPLE: <u>My favorite place in North Carolina is in the mountains.</u> I enjoy camping in the Black Mountains especially around Mount Mitchell. The camping is primitive, but let's me enjoy nature. Asheville is a great city to visit there as well. It has several tourist attractions including the Biltmore Estate and gardens. Finally I enjoy hiking and driving through the Great Smokey Mountains where nature has been preserved and where the Cherokee nation has established a center to learn about its culture.

*3. **YOUR PAPER SHOULD END WITH A CONCLUSION PARAGRAPH.** This paragraph wraps up what you've just said. (Yes, it's a repeat!) Shortly restate your thesis statement. Then finally apply what you've just said into larger terms.

EXAMPLE: Through the years I've enjoyed the mountains and coast of North Carolina, as well as our nation's capital city. These locations are close by, affording me much time to visit and vacation. I would highly recommend the Great Smokey Mountains as well as the free museums of Washington to anyone considering great vacation spots.

PAPER TOPIC PRACTICE

*Directions: *Make a short brainstorm list and prepare a thesis statement for each of the following topics.*

____ 1. Global warming and landfills are deep concerns Americans have for their environment. Explain how recycling and energy use can change our product-consuming lifestyle.

____ 2. Millions of Americans eat out one or more times every day. What could be the effects of fast-food eating on Americans?

____ 3. Many street people wander the towns and cities of America. What are some ways our society could deal with this phenomena?

____ 4. Many kids are members of a family whose parents or parent work every day. This means kids from age eight and older are now latch-key kids (they come home and stay alone). Discuss how being a latchkey kid can affect the family or the children.

____ 5. You're in your home alone one night and you hear a window being broken on the other side of your house. You go to the nightstand and reach for your gun. . .How might gun control affect the personal lives of most Americans?

____ 6. Currently there is a movement among adults to buy a DVD player and HD television and stay at home watching television or movies rather than going out. What are the effects of this "couch-potato" movement?

____ 7. The AIDS epidemic has made some dramatic changes in American life. Discuss the effects the disease has had on American life.

____ 8. With the downturn in the economy, many adults must return to school to get more training, diplomas or degrees. What kind of changes to their lives must they make to "return to school"?

Organizing Your Note-cards

Before you begin your outline, you must organize your note-cards. You should begin to sort your cards into similar ideas or subtopics. (Yes, you're scrambling them; that's why you put the author's name or title at the top!)

Sit at your desk or a table and simply stack the cards in piles of similar information. You may find some that don't fit--put these aside for later.

Once you've got the piles completed, then go through each pile and make sure the information goes together. This is the time to resort the cards. If your piles are complete, then sort each pile into some logical order. You may want to "code" the cards with a one-word note at the top or even alphabets. For example, all notes on whale's young would be "A" and all cards on mating habits would be "B," or put "young" on the first set and "mating" on the second.

Then, put the piles into a logical order. Once you've stacked or put these together, you can decide which of the cards that didn't fit you can still use. Unfortunately, and it's hard, you may have to simply discard the information as not useful. If you have some interesting ideas about the topic or definitions or quotes that don't quite fit, use them in your introduction! So these may become the pile for your introduction. Now you're ready to put the piles into your outline. Your introduction pile becomes the introduction, and each successive pile becomes a new Roman numeral (II, III, IV, etc). The cards in each pile become A, B, C, and etcetera. Follow the format given on the next page.

Outline Format
RESEARCH PAPER

After you've taken notes, you are ready to organize your ideas into an outline. Use this format to outline your paper. Organize the note-cards according to your outline. You may need to go back and do more research if your outline has empty spots. You need to quote at least one source for each point made.

Thesis:

    I.   **Introduction**.
        A.   Story, intro remarks, definition, etc.
        B.   **Thesis**.

    II.   Topic sentence for supporting paragraph #1.
        A.
        B.
        C.

    III.Topic sentence for supporting paragraph #2.
        A.
        B.
        C.

    IV. Topic sentence for supporting paragraph #3.
        A.
        B.
        C.

Conclusion.
        A.   Concluding statement (restates thesis)
        B.   Opinion (new idea or solution)

**Remember each topic sentence should be one small piece of your thesis statement

Sample Outline: The Computer Has Arrived

Thesis: The everyday person cannot escape the arrival of the computer since it is an important part of our daily lives, education, and employment.

I. Introduction.
   A. Brief history.
   B. Thesis.

II. The computer affects our daily lives in many ways.
   A. The use of the computer in banking.
   B. The use of the computer in shopping.
   C. The use of the computer in health care.

III. The computer has become an important part of education.
   A. Elementary children learn to read by using computers.
   B. Computers organize libraries for schools.
   C. Computer processing is taught as an essential skill.

IV. Finally the computer has been integrated into all forms of employment.
   A. In sales and retail, computers tabulate and record sales.
   B. Mechanics use computers to analyze cars.
   C. Occupations in areas such as health, education, and manufacturing depend on the computer.

V. Conclusion.
   A. The computer has come to dominate daily living, education, and employment.
   B. We have taken a step into the future where life will not be possible without the computer. (Or: People must become computer literate to function in tomorrow's world.)

Time to Decide on Final Presentation

You will still need an outline and note-cards to finish your final presentation of your research.

You can choose one of the following (unless your instructor says otherwise).

❖ Typed paper. Go on to the rough draft, then do a final draft. Put all in a cover.

❖ Speech. Go on to the rough draft. You may want to put your speech on note-cards, but don't plan to read your speech!

❖ Powerpoint. This is part written paper and part speech, except you are putting it in a computer presentation.

See the following pages for the type presentation you are planning to complete. Whichever presentation you choose, you must include a bibliography.

THE ROUGH DRAFT

Once your outline is prepared and your note-cards organized, you're ready for the rough draft. A rough draft is just that, a rough, unpolished version of your paper. You're **now** writing in complete sentences and complete paragraphs.

If your outline is thorough, you should only have to fill in the details or supporting sentences. This is where your note-cards and quotes from books play a very important role. Make the notes on your cards into sentences. Put quotation marks around direct quotes you use. Never just insert a quote, but tell why it's important or who said it. Direct quotes should be footnoted or referenced inside the paragraph (See below). You should also reference numbers, dates, and facts! Make sure **all the details** or supporting sentences **relate directly** to the topic sentence of the paragraph where you use them.

Footnotes

Footnotes acknowledge the source of a quote. Here are three ways:

1. A footnote at the bottom of the page. Number consecutively. The footnote looks exactly the same as the bibliographic note but only includes the author's name, book title, and page number.[6]

2. The footnotes can be given all at once at the end of the paper. Make sure you include numbers in the body of your paper.

3. Internal referencing. Put the author's name and page number in parentheses at the end of the sentence that contains the quote. No numbers are required. (Jensen p. 233)

---

[6]Jenson, Mary. Doing the Research Paper. (Holt-Rhineholt Publishing: New York). 1999. p. 233.

Citation Quiz

This activity will help you figure out what you need to cite in your research so that you don't accidentally plagiarize and earn a zero for an assignment.

Directions: Read each scenario carefully and decide whether you would have to cite the information in your portfolio or not.

(adapted from Robert Harris's citation quiz in <u>The Plagiarism Handbook</u>, p. 143)

1. You interview your sister about her experiences as a small business owner, and you use her experiences in your portfolio.
   ☐ Have to cite it
   ☐ Do not have to cite it

2. From your own experience, you know that nurses are in demand.
   ☐ Have to cite it
   ☐ Do not have to cite it

3. You find a picture on the Internet that would make a great visual for your portfolio coversheet.
   ☐ Have to cite it
   ☐ Do not have to cite it

4. You begin your career reflection with the phrase "A penny saved is a penny earned."
   ☐ Have to cite it
   ☐ Do not have to cite it

5. You use the Occupational Outlook Handbook to research your career choice, and include a lot of the information but you put it in your own words.
   ☐ Have to cite it
   ☐ Do not have to cite it

6. You interview a student who is in the same program as you, but he or she attends another community college.
   ☐ Have to cite it
   ☐ Do not have to cite it

7. You survey the class about whether or not they have enjoyed this course, and you use the survey results in your reflection on the course.
   ☐ Have to cite it
   ☐ Do not have to cite it

Answers in glossary

The Introductory Paragraph

Your paper should begin with an introduction that makes the reader think about the topic on which you're writing. Warning! The introduction is not a long explanation of your thesis statement. This paragraph can begin with any of the following:

- a story
- a definition
- why this topic is important
- a description
- everyone has experienced . . .
- news media reports on the topic
- why this topic is important to you personally

You may use the information that you found in your research that doesn't quite fit the subtopics you've organized the rest of the research into. The **thesis statement** is located at the <u>end</u> of the introductory paragraph. Also, it is **never** a good technique to have a thesis or topic sentence that says, "I chose this topic…" or "this paper is about…"

Example 1:

Everyone's heard of the gangs that occupy and terrorized parts of the big cities, but few are aware that there is gang activity here in the smaller cities of North Carolina. There have been reports of gang-style murders and activities in cities such as Fayetteville and Durham. A "clubhouse" was found with gang markings in Fayetteville, and two women were found executed in a nearby county. There are three basic identifiable warning signs that gangs are nearby: crime, colors, and markings.

Example 2:

Maria is lonely sixteen year old whose family is all but abandoned her to the world. There is no love, no concern of her well-being. Then she meets Jay and Marcus who invite who to spend time with them. They go out cruising and drinking, stopping on occasion to beat up someone they see. Soon Maria is wearing a bright red bandanna. She has found the world of gangs where she is loved, protected and has belonging. There are three basic identifiable warning signs that gangs are nearby: crime, colors, and markings.

Remember, just like film-makers, you do **not** have to do the introduction first. Go ahead and work with the research you've got and the outline you've completed. You may be surprised by some inspiration you gain as you write the body of your paper!

One final note: Don't forget to end your paper with a **conclusion** that restates your thesis in some form. Use your conclusion to challenge your reader to consider what you've presented or to take action.

Study Skills Practice: Return to the topics/thesis practice page and choose one thesis and write three different introductions to a possible paper.

Proofreading and the Final Draft

Once you've finished the rough draft, you should **proofread** for any mistakes. After the next page is a list of common proofreading marks. If you are using a computer, use the spell checker, but beware that most computerized spell checkers will think all names are misspelled. In that case, choose "ignore" in the window. Print your rough draft and check over it on paper. Most writers cannot see the mistakes on a computer screen.

A final draft should be typed if possible. (See format on next page.) Include your outline and your bibliography. Use the following list to check your rough draft. A list of things to include on your final paper is at the end of this section.

WRITING CHECKLIST:

- ☐ Topic chosen/developed
- ☐ Brainstorm questions to answer
- ☐ Research and note-cards
- ☐ Outline
- ☐ Rough Draft(s)
- ☐ Bibliography
- ☐ Revise/proofread rough draft
- ☐ Final draft typed (include a cover page with title of your paper)
- ☐ Final proofread/edit of final draft
- ☐ Final draft turned in (Keep a copy on your USB drive and e-mail it to yourself if you need to print on campus or just to have a backup.)

Things to PROOFREAD FOR:

Good Writing

- ✓ Spelling
- ✓ Punctuation
- ✓ Capitals
- ✓ No fragments
- ✓ Subject-verb agreement
- ✓ Pronoun agreement or reference
- ✓ No comma splices or run-ons
- ✓ Consistent verb tense
- ✓ Point of view consistency
- ✓ No wordiness or repetitive writing

more on next page!

CONTENT

✓ Introduction
✓ Stayed on topic
✓ Supported topic with examples
✓ Internal citations of sources

✓ No irrelevant ideas
✓ Conclusion
✓ Outline
✓ Bibliography (All sources listed)

The Completed Paper

Your final draft should be typed, double-spaced (Use 12 or 14 size font/Times or Roman). Use the spell/grammar checker, BUT ALSO do a hard-copy check since your computer can't tell the difference between "to," "two," or "too" and other such words. Also, students often "see" what they think they wrote on the screen. Reading a hard copy will give the proofreader a clearer picture.

In a folder or binder, you should include the following items:

_ Title Page (with paper's title, your name, course title and date)
_ Outline
_ Final Draft (pages numbered)
_ Bibliography
_ Blank back page

Neatness counts! Timeliness is essential! Hand your paper in on time because some instructors do not take late papers or have penalties for late hand-ins. Never leave a paper in the classroom where your class meets; go to the instructor's office and put it under his/her door.

Resource: Go to http://owl.english.purdue.edu/ for great help in writing and grammar.

Proofreader's Marks

Here is a table of common marks used in editing:

Mark	Mistake	Example
≡	capitalize	john and i ate at chili's.
/	lowercase	Where did you ~~G~~o?
⁀‿	transpose	I you love.
‿⁀	transpose	G e r o g e
^	insert	I love you ^a lot.
V	insert	"What did you say?"
⊙	insert period	I love you⊙
X	Remove punctuation or other	I do not like you.x
ℓ	delete	I do ~~not~~ like you.
P	Make a paragraph	
RO	Run-on	I ate lunch you did not. RO
CS	Comma-Splice	I ate lunch, you went out. CS
Frag	Fragment	Running down the hall. Frag
# or /	Insert space	He works a/lot.
agr	agreement	He <u>are</u> here. s-v agr
POV	Point of view shift	Parents should bring <u>your</u> baby to the nursery. POV
No TS	Missing topic sentence	
◯	misspelling	I (luv) you.

Proofreading Practice

A. Find punctuation, capitalization, spelling and grammar errors in the following paragraph. Use proofreader's marks as you correct.

Superstition and credulity led to north americas last trials for witchcraft in 1692 in the little village of Salem massachusetts. The witchcraft scare began when a Negro slave girl, Tituba told some voodoo stories to some friends who had nightmares as a result. There are no such things as witches. Trials of Tituba and others were held before Judge Samuel Sewall and Cotton Mather a coloniel preacher, Who conducted the prosecution? The trial's lasted about one year during which women ninteen were tried convicted and executed however Judge Sewall later confessed that he thought his judgments had wrong been.

B. **More practice**.

The American War of independence lasted from 1775 too 1783. At the end of it thirteen ex-british colonys formed the United States of america. These colonists has already made there own local laws, but the parliament british kept control of financial matters, particularly trade. Parliament tryed imposing taxes, on newspapers, tea, paper, lead and paint, but had to all except the tea tax. Women had no right to vote On december 16, 1773, a band of colonists disguised as Indians boarded ships in Boston harbor and through cargoes of tea overboard. The Revolution begun!

How to Make an Oral Presentation

Many times you may be asked to present your research in an oral fashion. This is more than reading your paper. It should be given as a speech. Remember Winston Churchill's advice:

- Tell them what you're going to tell them.
- Tell them.
- Tell them what you told them.

Follow these simple steps for an oral presentation:

- Make note-cards. (You may be able to use your research cards.) Write the notes in **simple** lines in large letters.
- Order your cards (follow an outline).
- Practice giving your speech in front of a mirror. Watch your time! (3-5 minutes or whatever limit you've been given)
- Prepare visual aids such as a poster, handout, and/or Powerpoint.

As you give your presentation:

- Be on time and be prepared.
- Take a few deep breaths before you start.
- Put your name and topic on the board if you do not have visual aids.
- If you have visual aids, put these beside you to show.
- Use your note-cards as you speak, but don't just read!
- Speak loudly and carefully.
- Say "thank you" when you're finished.

Visual Aids:

- One large poster--not too busy/large letters or pictures or physical items to show
- Overheads (use 18-24 font size)
- Powerpoint Program (no more than 7 lines/slide)
- All aids should be easy to handle and visible to all your audience!
- Handouts with short points or additional information and sources

Bibliography:

- Your instructor will require a bibliography (usually annotated with short notes of what the source was about). Prepare this just as you would for a written paper.

PowerPoint Hints

- ➢ Use the Wizard if you're unfamiliar with this program! Just follow its directions.
- ➢ No more than seven lines / slide!
- ➢ Use 40+ size
- ➢ Intersperse some pictures.
- ➢ Follow the order in your outline.
- ➢ Don't just copy your note cards. Simplify or put in your own words.
- ➢ Have a bibliography slide. Reference direct quotes on the slide where they appear.
- ➢ Practice giving your presentation—practice not just reading the slides but giving additional comments and information.

ON CAMPUS HELP

Your instructor – Most instructors have made dozens of presentations with PowerPoint and are happy to be a resource for you. You may make an appointment for a face-to-face meeting, or you can email your presentation to them to get feedback.

Tutors in Your Campus Learning Center– For help with spelling, grammar, and general writing skills, you can take your printed slides to tutors in your learning center.

Lab Monitors in the Computer Labs – If using a computer on campus and you need help, a lab monitor may be able to help you solve small problems. Do not hesitate to ask him/her.

ONLINE HELP

Microsoft Office Online – This interactive online course explains how to create a PowerPoint presentation step-by-step. The Overview page says that it will take you 40-50 minutes to move through the lessons.

http://office.microsoft.com/training/Training.aspx?AssetID=RC011298761033&CTT=6& Origin=RC011298761033

PowerPoint in the Classroom – This silly but helpful website is organized according to topic. If you are relatively new to PowerPoint, you may want to take the interactive quiz before you begin to create your own presentation: **http://www.actden.com/pp/index.htm**

10 Dos and Don'ts of PowerPoint
This website includes information on making an oral presentation with PowerPoint, but the formatting suggestions will work for your assignment.

http://www.microsoft.com/smallbusiness/resources/technology/business-software/presenting-with-powerpoint-10-dos-and-donts.aspx

Appendix B
Computer Research and Communication

Checklist for Online Learners

Are you ready to take an online course? Look at the following checklist. You should have "yes" for most answers!

Yes	No	Skill
☐	☐	1. I have regular access to a computer with Internet access.
☐	☐	2. I have an email account.
☐	☐	3. I check my email everyday.
		4. I am familiar with the following computer operations:
☐	☐	a. Navigating the Internet
☐	☐	b. Creating & saving files to a hard drive, disk, or flash drive
☐	☐	c. Sending and receiving email attachments
☐	☐	d. Searching for information on the Internet
☐	☐	e. Using more than one window at a time
		5. I have regular access to the following software:
☐	☐	a. A word-processing program (preferably Microsoft Word)
☐	☐	b. An Internet browser (preferably Internet Explorer 6 or higher or Firefox 2 or higher)
☐	☐	c. Power Point
☐	☐	6. I have taken or tested out of an Introduction to Computers course. (This is not a requirement, but it can be helpful.)
☐	☐	7. I am able to commit four hours per week for this class.
☐	☐	8. I am willing to ask for help when I need it.
☐	☐	9. I am self-motivated and disciplined.
☐	☐	10. I am comfortable communicating in writing.
☐	☐	11. I enjoy reading.
☐	☐	12. I do not procrastinate when it comes to schoolwork or deadlines.

The Internet

Your server will give you access to search on the net--find "net search" and type in the information you seek (See the next page for very useful hints!).

Search engines to use:
- Google
- Ask
- Yahoo
- Bing

Sites have a "tag" at the end of their World Wide Web addresses (URL addresses). The organizations are:

.com	=	commercial	.edu	=	educational
.org	=	organization			institution
.gov	=	government	.net	=	network

The most reliable sources are gov, edu, and org. Double check the credentials of addresses with ".com." Beware of sites with a broken key in the bottom left corner. These sites are unsecure which means if you submit information or interact with the site you may submit private information that anyone can access.

You can copy information by choosing "save" under edit or highlighting it with your mouse and choosing "copy" under edit. You should immediately "paste" it into a word processing document. You may also print the information you see, but this can be very slow! MAKE SURE YOU DO NOT PLAGIARIZE! Give references and use as little "cut and paste" as possible. Too much can give the instructor the impression that you merely copied someone else's work!

Practice by looking at these sites:

www.whitehouse.gov

www.imdb.com

www.cfnc.org

www.un.org

www.unc.edu

www.bls.gov/oco/

Internet Search Helps

The Internet contains thousands of sites with tons of information, all of which you must sift through in order to find information that you "searched" for using a search engine. Here are some hints to help you narrow your search results.

1. Use Quotation Marks (Example: "Modern Dance"). This will put the terms together in any site found, rather than finding sites with either modern or dance.

2. Use Capital Letters for names and titles. (Example: President Richard Nixon)

3. Use Plus Signs (+) directly in front of a word that you want to appear on any Web page the search engine finds (movie + Titanic).

4. Use Minus Signs (-) in front of a word you don't want on a Web page. (Example: Horses -wild).

5. Use Title Searches. Type title or t with a colon in front of a word. This will find sites with the word in the title.

6. Use Pipe Signs (|) These will find your words when they are mentioned in the first sections together.

Web Search Practice

Type in a subject (your paper topic is great!) and choose a URL site to gather information. Fill out the following form.

1. Site's URL address:	
2. Search engine you used:	
3. Words you used in your search:	
4. Describe the site (include author and title)	
5a. Topic 1 discussed: Brief description:	
5b. Topic 2 discussed: Brief description:	
5c. Topic 3 discussed: Brief description:	
5d. Topic 4 discussed: Brief description:	
6. List 3 things you learned:	*a.* *b.* *c.*
7. I want to learn more about:	
8. List at least one "link" (URL address) you found at this site:	

*You can use this information by transferring it to note-cards for your paper!

Storage Media

When students do research and complete papers or other presentations, such as Powerpoint or speeches, they need to save their work on at least two other locations for storage. This backup process will allow them access on campus so they can turn work in when it's due.

LOCATION ONE: A student saves his/her work on the laptop or desktop computer at home. (NOT IN A COLLEGE LAB!)

LOCATION TWO: It is essential that every student has a backup location such as a USB flash drive. A flash drive is a portable device that can be used on most computers. This can be purchased at your college bookstore or any electronics retailer.

SAFE REMOVAL INSTRUCTIONS:

After you have saved your document or your computer, do a save-as and select your flash drive (often known as portable or removable storage). To remove your flash drive SAFELY, go to your Windows taskbar, look for the <Safely Remove Hardware> icon, right click icon and select <Safely Remove Hardware>. A window will open, select USB Mass Storage Device, click <STOP> then <OK>. You can now safely remove your flash drive. This prevents data loss or the corruption of your USB drive. *<info by Tim Stuart>*

LOCATION THREE: E-mail yourself the document. Now you can access the document in any college computer lab or class with Internet.

Finally, you may want to save your word-processed document as an <rtf> file (rich text format), so it can be opened with any word processor. After saving your document as usual, do a <save-as> and choose <rtf> under document type.

Database Research

Your college's library provides its students with access to scholarly databases for research projects and papers. The databases are often dedicated to a particular study area such as the *Westlaw Primary* for use by paralegal students or the *PsycARTICLES* database for students in psychology courses. Your instructor may require that you do a certain amount (or all) your research using these types of databases. These are different from the typical information you might find on the Internet because they are compiled with research and articles from professional experts in their fields.

Check to see if your library requires passwords to access the databases. You still must cite all information that you use! Avoid "cut and paste" when using, so that you do not plagiarize others' work. Don't be afraid to ask your librarians for help narrowing down information.

Check for special collections and "libraries" that your college's library may have set aside for coursework offered. These are often developed to help large number of students doing similar projects or research.

Finally, remember these are electronic to help provide large quantities of information without taking up shelf space in the library and to allow many students to do the research at the same time. Use your USB drive to save small amounts of the database articles you've research. You should be able to use your computer to "print" the item to your drive by choosing CUTEPDF printer in your printer window. Again, watch using this to "cut and paste." This should be used to give you quick access to information and make your work easier.

Use summary or paraphrasing to compile information you find in the database. Make sure the information is as exact as possible rather than just repeated large amounts of information in your paper—instructors are not impressed with lots of information; they prefer summaries or just a few specific details to support your research thesis.

Appendix C: Vocabulary Building

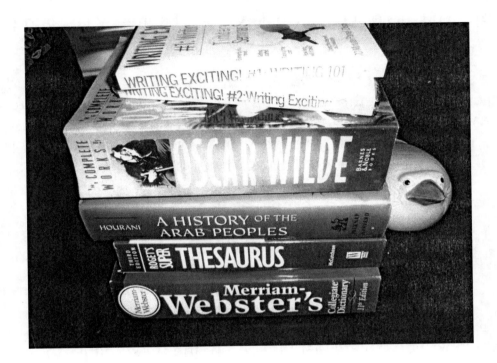

Additional Exercises to Increase Reading Skills

Vocabulary Study Introduction

One of the most basic skills you begin with in reading is VOCABULARY, or a list of words that will be used. You have a reading vocabulary, which is generally much larger than your speaking vocabulary, or what you use in language. Your listening vocabulary may be nearly as large as your reading.

Following are a series of very basic vocabulary skills. You will study how to use a dictionary and thesaurus as well as review basic word-building components such as suffixes and prefixes. You will review the parts of speech and begin to build your very own vocabulary. This is important because if you don't *own* a word, it won't be yours.

Making a word your own is as simple as this:

1. Write down the word at least five times.
2. Use the word every day for a week.
3. Look to read the word in your assignments or leisure reading.
4. Learn to spell the word.

Use the blank vocabulary list sheet on the next page to make your vocabulary. Good luck as you make your word power increase!

Reflection:

Do you read more than what you are required? If not, what are other ways to add to your vocabulary—both reading and writing?

My Vocabulary List

Class	Source: _lecture _book _research		Date	

WORD	TOPIC	DEFINITION	SENTENCE	KNOW IT!

Student permission to duplicate

Using a Dictionary

re-search (re´sûrch, resûrch´) *n*. Abbr. res. 1. Scholarly or scientific investigation or inquiry. 2. Close, careful study. —attributive. 1. Often used to modify another noun.

—**re-search** v. **re-searched**, **re-search-ing**, **re-search-es**.
—*intr*. 1. To engage in or perform research.
—*tr*. 1. To study (something) thoroughly so as to present in a detailed, accurate manner. 2. To do research for. —re-search-a-ble adj. — re-search-er or re-search-ist *n*.

This is a dictionary entry. Each word in the dictionary is called an entry. Note that the word is in a **boldface** type.

Next to each entry word is a pronunciation key in **parentheses** ( ). The **accent** mark / ´ / indicate which syllable is accented. Check the **pronunciation key** in the front of your dictionary to see how the letter symbols and marks affect pronunciation.

Next to the pronunciation of the word is the **part of speech**. These are usually abbreviated such as *n* for noun. Next the part of speech can be additional forms and/or abbreviations. In some dictionaries these come <u>after</u> all the definitions. Finally, the different **definitions** or meanings of the word are given.   Plurals and different verb tenses may also be given. There may be abbreviations to further explain the words origins or use. For example: colloq. = colloquialism / comp. = compound

At the top of each page are guide words which help you locate words alphabetically.

Using a Thesaurus

research *v*:   To go into or through for the purpose of making discoveries or acquiring information. look into, investigate, dig, explore, inquire, probe, scout, delve, reconnoiter.

A **thesaurus** is a book of synonyms, often including related and contrasting words and antonyms.

Like the dictionary it has its word entries in **boldface**. It is followed by the **part of speech**. There may be a **definition**. Finally there will be a choice of words that are **synonyms** (mean the same). In some thesauruses, there may be a list of **antonyms** (opposites) preceded by the abbreviation *ant*. Use your thesaurus in three main ways:

1.   To make new word choices when writing. The reader will be bored if you use the same word more than twice on a page.
2.   Like another dictionary. It will give you short simple definitions or a synonym you understand.
3.   To find the opposite. If you're writing and can't think of the opposite, then use your thesaurus.

Exercise/practice. *Find three synonyms and one antonym for each word. Use the word in a sentence and underline the synonym that can be used.*

Word	Synonym 1	Synonym 2	Synonym 3	Antonym
succeed				
Sentence:				
work				
Sentence:				
learn				
Sentence				

Parts of Speech

How a word acts in a sentence is its part of speech. The same word can have several parts of speech. Here is an example:

➢ I am *read*ing my textbook. (Reading is a verb.)
➢ *Reading* is fun! (Reading is a noun.)
➢ The *reading* class meets here. (Reading is an adjective.)

Part of Speech	Definition	Examples
Noun	A person, place, thing, idea or activity	Jackie, city, car, democracy, hiking
Verb	An action word or state of being	jump, sit, is, are, become
Pronoun	Takes the place of a noun	he, she, they, this, who, anyone
Adjective	Describes a noun or pronoun	Red, tall, great, helpful, charming
Adverb	Describes a verb, adjective or adverb	greatly, very, too
Preposition	Begins a prepositional phrase and always has an object	in, over, under, around, during, after
Conjunction	Joins words, phrases or sentences	for, and, nor, but, or, yet, so, however
Interjection	Shows emotion	wow, ouch, oh

Parts of Speech
Practice

Identify the part of speech for each underlined word:

1. The college has a large selection **of** curriculum programs available.
2. If you need to choose a career to study, you may **want** to speak to the counselor.
3. Durham **Technical** Community College was founded in the early sixties.
4. The college has increased **its** enrollment over the last thirty years.
5. The campus is located on Lawson Street **next** to **an** industrial area.
6. Are you interested in attending **or** just exploring the idea?
7. The president **of** the college is Dr. Bill Ingram, a **graduate** of NCSU.
8. "**Wow**!" is one way of describing the many facets of our college.
9. The college **student** will be a **graduate** then transfer to a university.
10. The class was overcome with **sudden** change of **schedule**.
11. **Their** instructor was **suddenly** overcome with sadness.
12. He spoke to the class **with** a loud, "**Aha**!"
13. We will **never** understand **how** the college **was** **affected**.
14. Students are concerned **about** the **effect** of **tuition** increases.
15. **Working** is quite difficult with a **very** full course **load**.

Challenge: Identify each of the words in the following sentence:

Unfortunately, the student did not see the DATA bus coming toward her, so she screamed loudly, "Ow!" as it swiped her leg.

Context Clues
A Key to Meanings

When you don't know the meaning of a word or phrase, there are several ways you can determine the meaning within the **context**, the part of a text or statement that surrounds it. Check for the following clues:

1. **Part of speech.** The part of speech will help determine the word's role. You may want to ask Is it doing the action or is it the action? Does it describe or indicate a place?

2. **Location.** Is the word highlighted or in bold letters? Is there a definition nearby? Look for an example or comma to show a phrase to define the word.

3. **Topic.** What is the subject of the sentence or paragraph? Does this word relate to it?

4. **Word parts and roots.** Look at prefixes or suffixes for meaning. Find the root or small word within the larger word.

5. **Same and opposite.** Look for a word that means the same (usually follows "or") in the sentence, or look for an opposite word.

Exercise: *Determine the meaning of each nonsense word, then write a synonym for it.*

1. I like to narf cards at night.
   The quarterback fumbled the ball in that last narf.
   We went to see a narf at the theater.   _____

2. We narlied the burgers on the grill.
   The narley fixed our salads.
   My dog only eats narlied meat.   _____

3. My husband sumkeed the kids while I worked.
   A sumkeed pot never boils.
   What time do you start you sumkee at the army base. _____

Contextual Practice:

Read these passages and answer the question that follows each.

Some animals practice a highly-developed type of adaptation when their habitats are changed by man's movement into natural areas. For example, squirrels will nest in attics or bears will eat from garbage cans.

What is *adaptation*? How did you determine this?

Many political leaders have attempted to create a utopian society for their followers; however, the imperfection of men and women has made this dream place nearly impossible.

What is a *utopia*?

Hydraulic technology has been a boon to most industries including engineering, energy production and manufacturing construction. This is why early in the Industrial Revolution plants and mills grew up along rivers and lakes.

What resource do *hydraulic* machines require?

Word Types

Words may play different roles in speech and writing. In each case, the word has a special designation or type.

synonym *n.* Abbr. *syn.* A word having the same or nearly the same meaning as another word or other words in a language. EXAMPLES:

hot--warm   lie down--recline
run--jog   wash--scrub

antonym *n.* Abbr. *ant.* A word having a meaning opposite to that of another word. EXAMPLES:

hot--cold   clean--dirty   search--find
run--walk   hope--despair   work--relax

homonym *n.* One of two or more words that have the same sound and often the same spelling but differ in meaning. EXAMPLES:

hear--here   pool--pull   see--sea
their--there   roe--row   to—too-two

jargon *n.* The specialized or technical language of a trade, profession, or similar group EXAMPLES:

COMPUTERS: hard drive/ PC/ memory/ROM
AUTOMOBILES: manifold/cruise/spoilers
FAST FOOD: fliers/to-go

slang *n.* A kind of language occurring chiefly in casual and playful speech, made up typically of short-lived coinages and figures of speech that are deliberately used in place of standard terms for added raciness, humor, irreverence, or other effect. EXAMPLES:

phat   bad
diss   word

cliché *n.* A trite or overused expression or idea.
    EXAMPLES: slow as molasses   sharp as a tack

(Word Types, cont'd)

acronym *n.* A word formed from the initial letters of a name. EXAMPLES:

> PC--personal computer   RAM--random access memory
> ATM—automatic teller machine   CD—compact disk
> 24/7—all the time
> WASP—white Anglo-Saxon Protestant (historical reference)

idiom *n.* A speech form or an expression of a given language that is peculiar to itself grammatically or cannot be understood from the individual meanings of its elements. EXAMPLES:

> keep tabs on _____
> make his mark _____
> raw deal_____
> come up with_____
> cold shoulder_____
> bosom buddies_____
> makes my blood boil_____
> hold the line_____
> tow the line_____
> give a piece of my mind_____
> bite his head off_____
> under the weather_____
> lay off_____
> a dime a dozen_____
> nest egg_____
> a New York minute_____
> a chip on your shoulder_____
> a blessing in disguise_____
> doozy_____
> once in a blue moon_____

> **Good websites to check:**
> ❖ http://www.idiomsite.com/
> ❖ http://www.idiomconnection.com/
> ❖ http://dictionary.cambridge.org/reference/roll.htm

Prefixes

Prefix *n.* *Abbr.* pref.   An affix, such as dis- in disbelieve, put **before** a word to produce a derivative word or an inflected form. Use prefixes to change the meaning of a word. Prefixes often make the new word opposite to the original form, such as *-dis* changing *belief* to <u>not belief</u>.

Here are few common prefixes and their meanings:

in	(not)	pro	(for)
re	(again)	pre	(before)
con	(against)	ex	(former)
de	(remove *or* reverse)	un	(not *or* reverse)
dis	(not)		
com	(together *or* with)		

EXERCISE:

Prefix +	Word =	New Word	Your Word
1. in-	complete		
2. un-	happy		
3. com-	promise		
4. re-	do		
5. con-	artist		
6. ex-	wife		
7. pre-	historic		
8. de-	toxification		
9. pro-	active		
10. dis-	continue		

ADD two words to your personal vocabulary list.

Suffixes

Suffix: *n. Abbr.* suff., suf. An affix added to the **end** of a word or stem, serving to form a new word or functioning as an inflectional ending. Suffixes can change a word from one part of speech to another. In some cases, a slight spelling change may be needed.

Noun endings

These suffixes change words into nouns. When you see a word with these endings, you can see it is a noun.

state or quality:	-ness, -ion, -ity, -ance, -ship, -hood
action or process:	-ment, -ion
one (person) that is:	-er (-or)
group that shares a quality or craft:	-hood, -ship
science, theory or study:	-logy

Practice:

Suffix +	Word =	New Word	Your Word
1. –er	write		
2. –ship	member		
3. –hood	brother		
4. –ology	criminal		
5. –ment	govern		
6. –ance	remember		
7. –ity	civil		
8. –ness	good		
9. –ion	commune		

*ADD three new words to your personal vocabulary list.

Suffixes
Part II

Suffix: *n. Abbr.* suff., suf.   An affix added to the **end** of a word or stem, serving to form a new word or functioning as an inflectional ending. Suffixes can change a word from one part of speech to another. Again, some spellings may change slightly.

Verb endings

These suffixes change words into verbs. When you see a word with these endings, you can see it is a verb.

-s   shows present tense for third person (he/she/it)
-ed   show past tense (watch for spelling changes)
-ing   shows action in progress in any tense (Note: sometimes used as a noun or gerund such as *Running* is fun.)
-en   participle form of verbs

EXERCISE:

Suffix +	Word =	New Word	Your Word
1. –s	write		
2. –ed	study		
3. –ing	jump		
4. –en	rise		

*Decide whether each underlined word is a noun or a verb. How can you tell?

    My favorite sport is <u>jogging</u>.
    We were <u>skiing</u> on Sugar Mountain.

*ADD two words that end in -en to your vocabulary lists.

Suffixes
Part III

Adjective endings

These suffixes change words into adjectives. When you see a word with these endings, you can see it is an adjective.

capable or susceptible to:	-able
characterized by:	-ous, -ic, -some
full or like:	-ful
relating to or like:	-ish, -like
without or lacking:	-less
comparative forms:	-er (two), -est (three or more)

Adverb endings

The -ly suffix changes words into adverbs. Watch for spelling changes since it often added to words that end in -y. It means *like* or *in a manner of*.

EXERCISE:

Suffix	Word =	New Word	Your Word
1. –ly	happy		
2. –ic	class		
3. –less	penny		
4. –ous	marvel		
5. -able	live		
6. –ish	child		
7. –like	child		
8. –some	trouble		
9. –ful	help		

-ER or- EST? (Use with *happy*.) John is <u>happ   </u> than his sister, but his sister is the <u>happ   </u> girl on the street.

*ADD three adjectives to your vocabulary list!

Suffixes
Part IV

Nouns /Adjectives Endings

These endings can make words into nouns or adjectives. Watch how the word is used in the sentence in order to figure out which part of speech it is.

Ending	Noun meaning	Adjective meaning
-ant or –ent	One that performs	State or condition
-al or –ent	Action or process	Characterized by

EXERCISE:

Suffix +	Word =	New Word	Your Word	Noun or Adj.
1. –ent	precede			
2. –ant	serve			
3. –ent	persist			
4. –al	hymn			
5. –ant	discord			
6. –al	nation			

Prefix and Suffix Practice

Add a prefix and/or a suffix to each word.   See how many you can add!

friend	handle	revere
allow	interest	work
boy	form	wild
girl	fun	lead
consist	marry	employ
decide	love	sex
courage	sane	relate
compute	find	success
hear	settle	study

Confusing Words

There are some commonly misspelled and misused words students often have trouble with. Study the list and use it when you have trouble!

then	shows time (conj)
than	compares (v)
it's	it is (abbrev)
its	possessive of it (pro)
except	an exclusion (adv)
accept	to receive (v)
effect	a result (n)
affect	to make a change in (v)
all ready	prepared (adj)
already	previously (adv)
they're	they are (abbrev)
their	possessive of they (pro)
there	place (adv)
sit	to seat oneself (v)
set	to put an object (v)
lie	to recline (v)
lay	to put down (v)
aid	to help (v)
aide	a helper (n)
among	amid several (prep)
between	amid two items (prep)
like	have similarities (adv)
for example	a sample (phrase)
alright	*misspelling—don't use*
all right	good or okay (adj)
to	direction (prep)
too	also or amount (adv)

Greek Roots/ Affixes

There are common roots and affixes that are useful to learn. These will help you break words into smaller parts to discover their meanings.

Root or Affix	Meaning	Find a Word
a	without	
acou, acu	to hear	
amphi	on both sides	
anthro	man, mankind	
anti	against	
auto	self	
bi	two	
biblio	book	
bio	life	
cent	100	
chron	time	
circum	around	
com	put together	
dec	ten	
dia	across	
eu	good	
gen	kinds, race, origin	
geo	earth	
graph	write	
helio	sun	
hetero	different	
homo	same	
hydro	water	
inter	among or between	
intra	within	
log	word	
meter	measure	
multi	many	
mono	one	
patho	disease	
poly	many	
sub	before	
tele	at a distance	
trans	across or beyond	

Latin Word Roots/Affixes

Root or Affix	Meaning	Find a Word
ante	before	
aqua	water	
audio, aur	hear/ear	
bene	well	
cap, cipt, cept	take	
carn	flesh	
cord	heart	
corpus	body	
credo	belief	
dorm	sleep	
duc, duct	lead	
ego	I, self	
locus	place	
mit	send	
mortis, mort	dead	
pater	father	
port	carry	
sanguin, sangui	blood	
solus	alone	
somn	sleep	
son	sound	
utilis	useful	
video	see	

Testing Vocabulary

Testing can have a language all of its own. The directions or question may use words not usually found in other readings. Learn this list to improve your testing skills!

according
analyze
argument
chronological
comparison
completion
computation
compute
contrast
definition
demonstrate
directions
discuss
essay
evaluate (evaluation)
example
example
explanation (explain)
illustrate
illustration

implication
indicate
instructions
interpret
interpretation
matching
multiple answer
multiple choice
outline
passage
Scantron
short answer
situation
solution
specific
statement
strategy
succinct
vocabulary

More Words to Learn

abeyance
affable
allegory
ampersand
assuage
augur
banal
brouhaha
cache
cacophony
callow
censorious
circumflex
claque
coda
cognizant
contiguous
corrigendum
credible
criterion
cull
cursory
de facto
decipher
deem
defer
defunct
deplete
deride
detrimental
deviate
digress
discerning
discordant
discrepancy

e.g.
edifice
effect
efficacious
elegy
eminent
ensue
epitome
erroneous
et. al.
ethnocentricity
evade
excerpt
explicit
extraneous
facsimile
fallacy
faux
fluctuate
fluency
forte
furor
futurism
gist
grapple
harbinger
heresy
homogeneous
hovel
hybrid
i.e.
ideogram
idiosyncrasy
idyllic
ilk

imminent
impromptu
inadvertent
incongruous
indignant
inert
insidious
intangible
intersperse
itinerary
jeopardize
juncture
lackadaisical
laudable
leery
libel
lieu
Machiavellian
malapropism
mete
milieu
moniker
nebulous
nepotism
nihilism
nondescript
palindrome
parody
pernicious
perquisite
phraseology
pithy
precedence
prevalent
pundit

quell
rapport
redundant
reiterate
remiss
repercussion
resilient
retort
satire
schism
sequential
snafu
staunch
stopgap
subliminal
subsequent
succinct
sustenance
tacit
taut
tentative
terse
transient
ubiquity
ulterior
uncanny
unconscionable
unequivocal
unprecedented
upshot
vapid
veracious
veracity
virtually
volition

Selected words from Michelle Bevilacqua *More Words You Should Know*

Appendix D Forms

Goal Setting/Accomplishment
Mapping
Time Analysis Grids
Assignment Sheets
Things-to-do Lists
Venn Diagram
Note-card Form
Class Contacts

Students are given express permission to **copy** forms **in this section**.

Goal

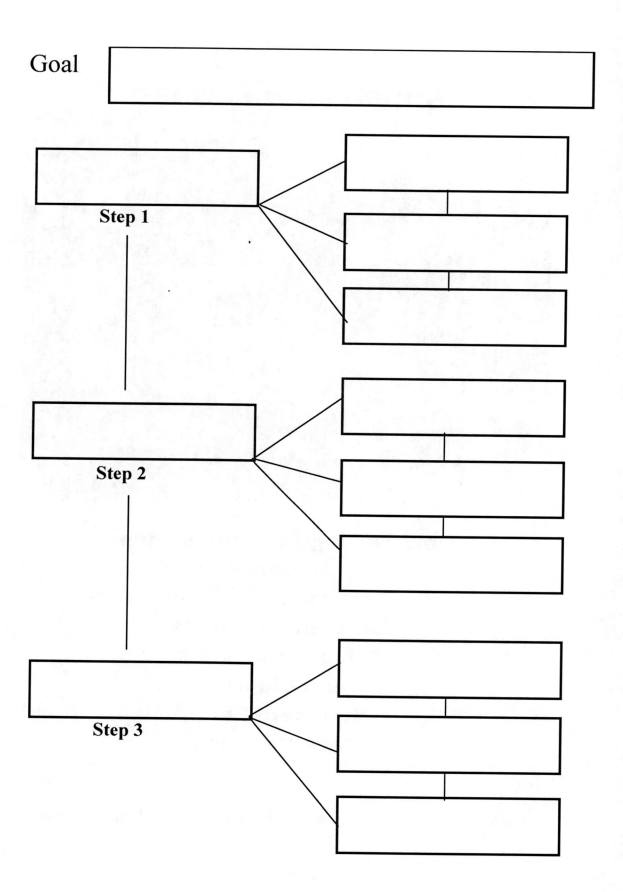

Assignment List

Date Received	Date Due	Assignment	Type	Done √
			☐ handout ☐ text p.___	
			☐ handout ☐ text p.___	
			☐ handout ☐ text p.___	
			☐ handout ☐ text p.___	
			☐ handout ☐ text p.___	
			☐ handout ☐ text p.___	
			☐ handout ☐ text p.___	
			☐ handout ☐ text p.___	
			☐ handout ☐ text p.___	
			☐ handout ☐ text p.___	
			☐ handout ☐ text p.___	
			☐ handout ☐ text p.___	
			☐ handout ☐ text p.___	
			☐ handout ☐ text p.___	
			☐ handout ☐ text p.___	
			☐ handout ☐ text p.___	
			☐ handout ☐ text p.___	

Students have permission to photocopy this page.

Things-to-Do Lists

Priority Rating	TASK	done		Priority Rating	TASK	done		Priority Rating	TASK	done

✂ Cut the 3 lists apart!
Permission for student to duplicate

Weekly Time Analysis Worksheet
Part 1: SPECULATE what you plan to do for the next week!

	Monday	Tuesday	Wednesday	Thursday	Friday	Saturday	Sunday
midnight							
1:00 a.m.							
2:00 a.m.							
3:00 a.m.							
4:00 a.m.							
5:00 a.m.							
6:00 a.m.							
7:00 a.m.							
8:00 a.m.							
9:00 a.m.							
10:00 a.m.							
11:00 a.m.							
noon							
1:00 p.m.							
2:00 p.m.							
3:00 p.m.							
4:00 p.m.							
5:00 p.m.							
6:00 p.m.							
7:00 p.m.							
8:00 p.m.							
9:00 p.m.							
10:00 p.m.							
11:00 p.m.							

Weekly Time Analysis Worksheet
Part 2: RECORD the ACTUAL activities of your week.

	Monday	Tuesday	Wednesday	Thursday	Friday	Saturday	Sunday
midnight							
1:00 a.m.							
2:00 a.m.							
3:00 a.m.							
4:00 a.m.							
5:00 a.m.							
6:00 a.m.							
7:00 a.m.							
8:00 a.m.							
9:00 a.m.							
10:00 a.m.							
11:00 a.m.							
noon							
1:00 p.m.							
2:00 p.m.							
3:00 p.m.							
4:00 p.m.							
5:00 p.m.							
6:00 p.m.							
7:00 p.m.							
8:00 p.m.							
9:00 p.m.							
10:00 p.m.							
11:00 p.m.							

Venn Diagram

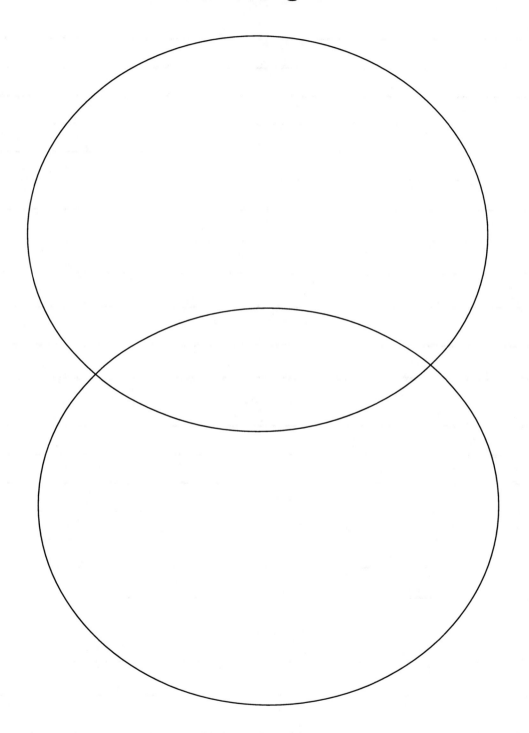

Notecard Practice Sheet

My Semester Plan

Semester 1 (Semester and Year: _____)

Courses	Credit Hours	Contact Hours

Semester 2 (Semester and Year: _____)

Courses	Credit Hours	Contact Hours

Semester 3 (Semester and Year: _____)

Courses	Credit Hours	Contact Hours

Semester 4 (Semester and Year: _____)

Courses	Credit Hours	Contact Hours

Semester 5 (Semester and Year: _____)

Courses	Credit Hours	Contact Hours

Semester 6 (Semester and Year: _____)

Courses	Credit Hours	Contact Hours

Semester 7 (Semester and Year: _____)

Courses	Credit Hours	Contact Hours

Semester 8 (Semester and Year: _____)

Courses	Credit Hours	Contact Hours

Class Contact Sheet

Get the names and contact info for a few students in each of your class. Use these contacts to get assignments, compare notes or form study groups!

Name	E-mail	Phone	Class We Share

*Be polite! Don't give out numbers for social reasons or use them for socializing (unless given permission). Keep this list in a **safe** place. <u>Shred</u> it when the semester is done.

Appendix E

Glossary of Terms

Durham: A small city in North Carolina.
Technical: Having to do with specialized careers.
Community: A designated group that lives or works together.
College: An institution of higher learning (beyond secondary).

Basic Skills: Programs for reading, math and language instruction.

Acute Stress	Results from demand and pressures of recent past or anticipation of future demands and pressures.
Advisor	Your assigned academic advisor in the field in which you are studying. Can be an instructor. Students not declared or accepted into their fields of study may be given a temporary advisor.
Anxiety	Feeling of apprehension or fear that has physical symptoms such as palpitations and sweating
Associate in Applied Science	Completion of all required courses as listed on the specific program's plan of study totaling no fewer than 64 semester hour credits. The degree prepares students for a particular career.
Associate in Arts	Completion of all requirements for the Associate in Arts degree totaling 64 semester hour credits. A degree with an emphasis on courses such as English, fine arts, foreign languages, history, philosophy, psychology, or sociology.
Associate in General Education	Completion of all requirements for the Associate in General Education degree totaling 64 semester hour credits. A two-year degree designed for individuals wishing to broaden their education, with emphasis on personal interest, growth and development.
Associate in Science	Completion of all requirements for the Associate in Science degree totaling 64 semester hour credits. Degree emphasizes science programs such as biology or chemistry.
Attitude	How you deal with conflict and how you approach your classes, assignments and interactions. This is shown by your eye contact and movement, body language, and verbal expression.
Bachelor's	Degree earned at a 4-year institution that generally requires 124+ semester hours.
Balance	A biological system that enables us to know where our bodies are in the environment and to maintain a desired position.
Bibliography	A list of sources used in paper or project. May need to follow MLA or APA format.
Bilateral agreements	Transfer agreements for AAS programs which are not designed for transfer such as computer classes that transfer to Appalachian State but not to NCSU
Blog	An online journal. Comes from web + log = blog. Go to blogspot.com for seeing examples or setting up your own.
Break	This could mean a semester break in the middle of the semester or could indicate a short break in the middle of your individual class time. Check with your instructor.
Calendar	A personal planner or larger display of the months and days of a year. Vital to help students stay current with assignments and tests.

Certificate	Completion of all required courses identified on the program's plan of study totalir 18 semester hour credits.
Capacity	How the body deals with stress. This can be healthy or unhealthy
Center for Academic Excellence	A place to get tutored. Check the hours your CAE is open.
Chronic Stress	Occurs when life is a year-after-year grind that wears on a person's health.
Colleague number	The number assigned to each student. NOT his/her social security number.
College ID	A student's identification card which serves as an identification that he or she belongs on campus. Can also get student discounts at local businesses. May serve as the library card.
College Transfer	See University Transfer.
Commencement	The graduation ceremony for a college. May be held several times a year. Requires specific regalia (dress) and procedure.
Community College	An educational institution that provides education for associate degrees (AA), certificates and diplomas for technical, business, or medical careers. These colleges are often 2-year institutions where there is no campus living. Also, they tend to be cost-efficient.
Comprehensive Articulation Agreement	Agreement between NC community colleges and UNC-system institutions to protect transfer students
Co-operative learning	Educational assignments or projects done with a group in a class. Teaches teamwork for the workplace.
Co-oping	Internships where students gain work experience in their chosen field of study. Usually unpaid and student must register for this experience.
Co-requisite	A course taken or done at the SAME TIME.
Dean	A director of a series of programs such as the dean of student affairs or the dean of liberal arts.
Department Chair	A lead instructor or faculty member who directs a department or program.
Developmental education	Course designed to improve a college student's skills. These include reading, writing and math. Generally a student is required to take these courses FIRST before he or she can enroll in his/her field of study. Course numbers are below 100 and do not transfer and are not figured into the student's major GPA.
Diploma	Completion of all required courses identified on the program's plan of study totaling no fewer than 36 semester hour credits. The adult high school program's diploma is equivalent to 21 units. The GED is a high school equivalency diploma.

Discussion Board	Like a chat room but an academic place to interact with instructors and students. Not a place to socialize or use profane language.
Drop-Add	A designated day on which students may change their class schedules by withdrawing (drop) or adding courses. This may require approval from an advisor. Generally this day occurs so students do not pay for courses dropped.
E-mail	An essential tool for communicating with instructors. Get your free e-mail at www.gmail.com.
Episodic Stress	Occurs in short-term events such as a near accident.
Episodic-Acute Stress	Reactions include being over-aroused, short-tempered, irritable, anxious, and tense. Often, described as having "a lot of nervous energy." Always in a hurry.
ESL	English as a second language. Courses in English for foreign speakers.
Etiquette	How someone acts in a specific setting or event. It could be called manners and includes not disrupting a class with disrespect, profane language, ringing or vibrating cell phone or its use, being prepared, cooperating with the instructor as well as arriving on time and leaving when dismissed (and not packing up until the instructor dismisses you).
FAFSA	Free Application for Federal Student Aid. All students submit this to determine what aid they qualify for. Go to www.fafsa.ed.gov for more information.
Fees	Money that covers facilities, parking, services, organizations and lab materials.
FERPA	Family Education Right to Privacy Act. Federal law that protects a student's information and grades. No information or grades can be given to someone else without student's permission which includes employers or parents. Instructors cannot e-mail or phone grades.
Field of Study	The educational program that trains a student in the career he or she has chosen. This may include university transfer where he or she will go to a 4-year college and major in a bachelor's degree program or major.
Financial Aid	Loans, grants and scholarships for student needs such as tuition, fees, books and living expenses. Students must fill out the FAFSA.
Frantic	How a student feels sometimes when an assignment is due and he or she has not started it. Avoid Frantic by not **procrastinating**. (See glossary for this term).
Goals	Something desired. Make take planning and much work to achieve. Set short-term goals often. Use SMART goals: specific, measurable, attainable, realistic, timely. Go to http://www.topachievement.com/smart.html for more information.

GPA	Grade point average. This is arrived at by taking the # of classes your are taking of credit hours for each) and add them together. Take the grade you receive and multiply its point value (A=4 B=3 C=2 D=1 F/F2=0). Add these quality points together and divide by the # of classes you take. 3 credit hours X grade pts = quality pts earned Quality pts for each course added together then divided by how many classes taken = GPA.
Highlighter	A yellow (or other translucent color) pen used to mark in a textbook. It is acceptable to highlight your text even if you plan to resell it. Highlight essential definitions and points or one example. Do not color your page.
Holland Code	An inventory that matches personality and skills to career paths.
Hybrid	A hybrid course requires BOTH online and physical attendance in a classroom. Generally doesn't meet as often as a standard, on-site class although the students MUST meet for the first class! Special permission may be needed and students must have an Internet-ready computer.
Inventory	A "test" that allows someone to gain a stronger sense of skills or attitudes or preferences in behavior. LASSI and VARK are inventories. Generally there is no grade for these, but the instructor might grade for completing it.
Journal	Unlike a personal diary, a journal in the educational setting is generally assigned topical writings. Ask your instructor how long each entry should be and how often you should enter these. Could be an online blog.
Kinesthetic	A learning style when someone learns by touching or doing.
Lab course	A learning and doing class that accompanies another course. Students must attend and pass both the lab and the regular class to get credit. May be scheduled at a different time from the regular class.
Learning style	How a person learns. Various inventories define these styles in multiple ways, but the three basic are Visual (see), auditory (speak or hear), and kinesthetic (touch or do). Try the VARK to determine yours. Use it often.
Library Card	See college ID
Major	A course of study in college. The college sets courses to complete the major and award the degree associated with that major (such as arts or science).
Make-up Testing	If a student misses a class's test or exam, this may be substituted. BEWARE! Many instructors do not do make-up testing for tests or exams, so contact them before you miss. Be prepared to validate your absence with a doctor's note, lawyer's letter or other legal documentation. Pop quizzes are not usually allowed to a make-up.
Margin	The edge of a paper. Should be set at an inch in word-processing documents.
Mentor	A student or instructor who helps support students and their classes.

Mission statement	The values and goals that direct an institution or an individual and is reflected in what is accomplished or achieved.
NS	No show which designated a student never attended a course.
Objective	The goal for a course. Could also be the opposite of subjective when a question has a clear right or wrong answer and does not rely upon anyone's opinion.
Online course	A course that is taken strictly online. Time is tracked through the computer program used for this instruction (such as Blackboard). Usually good for very self-disciplined student. Has exact time deadlines for assignment completion. May be given in a computer lab or learning center setting.
Open lab	A computer lab that has hours when students can come and use computers. Students should have their college ID cards to check in.
Plagiarism	Act of cheating or stealing. This includes not documenting information for any project. Documentation is generally done internally or by footnoting and accompanied by a bibliography at the end. See your library or instructor for details. A serious offense and will earn a zero on the assignment or for the course.
Plan of Study	The list or plan of courses a student must follow in order complete requirements in a course of study or major at a college.
Planner	A calendar designed for students. Usually each college has its own planner which can be purchased in the campus bookstore.
Pop Quiz	An unannounced (usually) short test on the reading assignment or prior notes or learning experience.
Portfolio	A collection of essays, documents or other. In this course, your portfolio is a collection of items about your possible career--you can treat each individually, but must include a table of contents and page numbers.
Poster	Used in the professional arena at conferences to present information where your audience comes and goes and you present as they come. It is used in place of a speech or presentation.
Pre-major agreements	listings of courses developed by NC university and community college faculty and then specified for a specific community college's students
Preregistration	Signing up for classes early or before the next semester starts. Vital to see your advisor before the registration lines open.
Pre-requisite	A course or test required BEFORE taking a new course or doing an assignment.
President	Highest director of a college.

Priority	Something done first. Prioritizing will help the student get assignments done. Of course, your education should be high on your list of priorities but don't neglect other life priorities.
Procrastinate	To put off or delay unnecessarily. Procrastination leads to stress and frantic behavior. Use your calendar and prioritize assignments. For large assignments, break up the work into smaller doable chunks. Use your rubric to check off each part as you complete it.
Program director	Directs a program in a department. Usually supervises the instructors in that program.
Quality points	What a student earns in his/her course grade. It is calculated by the number of credit hours multiplied by the grade. A=4; B=3; C=2; D=1 and F/F2=0.
Registrar	College personnel who manage course registration. Often just a referral to the "office." Place to go for adding or withdrawing from courses. Handles transcripts.
Response	Stress as a result of being exposed to a stressor.
Resume	A document for employers that gives work experience and education background of a potential employee.
rtf	Rich text format. Save your documents in this form if you do not have the college's word processing program. DTCC uses MS Word. E-mail yourself a copy so that you have access on campus to print.
Rubric	A list of grading for any assignment. Generally tells the student what points the instructor gives or takes away. This helps the instructor stay objective.
Satellite sites	Places where a college holds classes that are not on its main campus.
Scavenger Hunt	Looking for information or knowledge. (Not the kind where one runs about gathering odd items, but can require photos or materials brought back to complete.)
Security	Campus police. Report incidents to them or get a safe escort to your vehicle. Make sure you have your ID card with you and a parking permit. Your student fees pay for these.
Stress	Stimulation of anxiety caused by procrastination or other life factors. Generally considered a bad thing to experience. Try to plan and also take time to relax.
Stressor	Any event or situation that is perceived by an individual as a threat causing us to either adapt or initiate the stress response.
Study tracks	Listings of courses either recommended by DTCC faculty as appropriate for a degree or developed in collaboration with a particular NC college

Syllabus	The semestrial plan of events for a class; includes rules and vital information for a course.
Time management	How a student plans and carries out his/her schedule of education pursuits, jobs, and family/personal needs. Should be carried out by using a calendar or planner, daily schedule, prioritizing and executing the plan. Procrastination is the opposite of time management.
Transfer	To move from one place to another. This can refer to moving courses (if a college accepts them) or a student who moves from the community college to the university or 4-year college. Generally community college students work in the university transfer program.
Tuition	Money paid to take classes. Due before classes begin. In-state means the student is a resident of the state for at least one year. Out-of-state tuition is much higher because each state supplements funds.
Tutorial	A session where a tutor (teacher) helps students with skills they need for a class. Tutors do not complete assignments. Students should go to the Center for Academic Excellence to get tutored, but they should arrive having tried the work first. Not a substitute for attending class.
Undergraduate	The students enrolled in a bachelor's degree program.
University Transfer	The program you are enrolled in to earn either an associates in arts or sciences (for whichever major area you will study is more heavily emphasized). Also known as college transfer. Visit the Transfer Center in Phillips Building!
Values	Those beliefs that a person finds useful and follows in his/her choices. These may change through a person's life events and are influenced by family, peers, society, media, education, religion and life-events. A college also has values. Go to the website **www.durhamtech.edu/html/prospective/geninfo.htm#mission** to see a college's values.
VARK	A learning style inventory. Determines the way a student learns best. Go to the website: http://www.vark-learn.com/english/page.asp?p=questionnaire
VENN diagram	Two circles drawn to intersect in the middle. The outer edges are information about two different things (in this case careers or specialties) as they are DIFFERENT; the intersecting middle is what they have in COMMON.
Withdraw	To formally take oneself out of a course. Check your college's deadlines. If a student does not withdraw in a timely manner, the instructor will assign an F or F2 as the grade.
Work-study	Programs at colleges that place students in jobs (on or off campus) to earn money while attending classes. May be connected with financial aid awards.

X	Item or answer is wrong. An error.
Yearn	To desire. To really want this. Students should yearn for good grades and succes as well as knowledge.
Yerkes-Dodson Principle	The idea that certain amount of stress is good for an individual.
Zamboni	An ice-making machine to maintain ice in a hockey rink. Go see one at a game to relax and de-stress.
Zoology	A great course in animal biology.

Instructor: One who facilitates learning.

Answers to Critical Thinking Fun

Down in the dumps	Head over heels	A sock in the eye	Ring around the rosie
Sunday afternoon	88 Keys on a piano	Double cross	A pair of pants
Looking backwards	Misunderstanding	Double exposure	24 hours in a day
Life begins at forty	In between jobs	A big laugh	All mixed up
You don't bury SURVIVORS!			
Not a math problem—you have two apples!			

Answers to Sample Test Questions

Multiple Choice Samples
1. a   2. a   3. c   4. c

True-False Samples

All examples are *false*

Citation Quiz

#2 and 4—do not have to cite
All others you do have to cite!

Stressful Terminology
Anxiety 3K
Balance 5B
Stress 1C
Capacities 8A
Yerkes-Dodson 2F
Stressor 10 E
Response 9I
Episodic Acute 4H
Acute 6J
Chronic 7D

Appendix F

List of Resources Used in Textbook

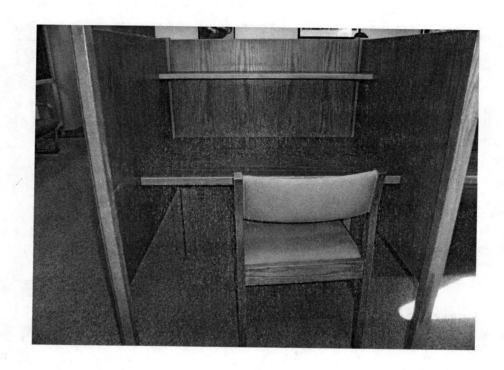

Citations List

We gratefully acknowledge these sources in putting together this textbook.

Bevilacqua, Michelle. *More Words You Should Know.* (Adams Media Corporation). 1989.

Brian, Tracy. *Eat That Frog!* Berrett-Koehler Publishers; 2nd edition (2007).

Career Key. Website: www.careerkey.org

Clarke, Jean Illsley. *Self-Esteem: A Family Affair.* (Winston Press) 1978.

Durham Technical Community College. Website: www.durhamtech.edu

Holmes, T.H.; Rahe, R.H. "The Social Readjustment Scale." *Campus Health Guide.* Carol Otis and Roger Goldingay. (New York: 1989).

Hopper, Carolyn H. *Practicing College Learning Strategies* (4th ed.) Wadsworth Publishing. 2006.

Jenson, Mary. *Doing the Research Paper.* (Holt-Rhineholt Publishing: New York). 1999.

King, Jr., Martin Luther. "I Have a Dream." Speech given August 28, 1963.

Lombardi, Vince; Baucom, John. *Babysteps to Success.* (Starburst Publications). 1997.

North Carolina's Career Resource Network. Website: www.soicc.state.nc.us.

Rubio, Paula, et. al. Content adapted from an article in the *Journal of Counseling and Development*: "The Wheel of Wellness Counseling for Wellness: A Holistic Model for Treatment Planning" (2000) by Jane E. Myers, Thomas J. Sweeny, and J. Melvin Witmer.

Stock, Gregory. *The Book of Questions.* (1985)

Wisconsin Vocational Studies Center, University of Wisconsin at Madison. *Puzzled About Educating Special Needs Students?*

About the Author...

Janice Stuart graduated from the University of North Carolina at Greensboro with a Bachelor's of Arts in both English and History. She earned a Master's of Education in Adult and Community College Education with a specialty in Reading from North Carolina State University. She has taught reading, English, social studies, GED preparation, and study skills for over 20 years. She has taught for Durham Tech since 1993. In 1990, she published a curriculum to teach basic survival skills for the homeless for the state of North Carolina. She has published two other texts on study skills (1998, 2000) and two English texts, *English Grammar for Writing* (2008) and *Grammar for Basic Education* (2009). In her "free" time, she enjoys writing science fiction and fantasy, crocheting baby blankets and walking with her husband and terriers.

About the Special Contributor...

Gabby McCutchen coordinates and teaches College Success at Durham Technical Community College. Gabby has worked at Durham Tech since 2004, and is the 2007 recipient of the Excellence in Teaching Award. She holds a Master's Degree in Teaching English to Speakers of Other Languages and a Bachelor's Degree in English. When she isn't teaching or taking classes herself, she enjoys home improvement projects, college football, and reading.